REVISED
EDITION

The Arrow Book of
STATES

By MARGARET RONAN

Illustrated by William Meyerriecks

Maps by Frank Ronan

Designed by Mary Jane Dunton

SCHOLASTIC BOOK SERVICES

NEW YORK · TORONTO · LONDON · AUCKLAND · SYDNEY · TOKYO

STATES AND THEIR ABBREVIATIONS

	Old	*New**		*Old*	*New**
Alabama	Ala.	AL	Montana	Mont.	MT
Alaska	None	AK	Nebraska	Nebr.	NE
Arizona	Ariz.	AZ	Nevada	Nev.	NV
Arkansas	Ark.	AR	New Hampshire	N.H.	NH
California	Calif.	CA	New Jersey	N.J.	NJ
Colorado	Colo.	CO	New Mexico	N. Mex.	NM
Connecticut	Conn.	CT	New York	N.Y.	NY
Delaware	Del.	DE	North Carolina	N.C.	NC
Florida	Fla.	FL	North Dakota	N. Dak.	ND
Georgia	Ga.	GA	Ohio	None	OH
Hawaii	None	HI	Oklahoma	Okla.	OK
Idaho	None	ID	Oregon	Oreg.	OR
Illinois	Ill.	IL	Pennsylvania	Pa.	PA
Indiana	Ind.	IN	Rhode Island	R.I.	RI
Iowa	None	IA	South Carolina	S.C.	SC
Kansas	Kans.	KS	South Dakota	S. Dak.	SD
Kentucky	Ky.	KY	Tennessee	Tenn.	TN
Louisiana	La.	LA	Texas	Tex.	TX
Maine	Me.	ME	Utah	None	UT
Maryland	Md.	MD	Vermont	Vt.	VT
Massachusetts	Mass.	MA	Virginia	Va.	VA
Michigan	Mich.	MI	Washington	Wash.	WA
Minnesota	Minn.	MN	West Virginia	W. Va.	WV
Mississippi	Miss.	MS	Wisconsin	Wis.	WI
Missouri	Mo.	MO	Wyoming	Wyo.	WY

These new abbreviations were approved in 1963 by the Post Office Department. They will gradually replace the old abbreviations.

PHOTO CREDITS — pp. 108-109: U.P.I., Maine State Highway Commission, Log Cabin Syrup, General Dynamics Corp.; pp. 110-111: Port of New York Authority, Wheaton-Monkmeyer, U.S. News & World Report, Shell Oil Co., U.S. Steel; pp. 112-113: Bloom-Monkmeyer, Live Stock Photo Co., International Harvester Co., Pace-Monkmeyer, General Motors; pp. 114-115: The New York Times, De Wys, Kentucky Chamber of Commerce, Standard Oil of N.J., Twentieth Century Fund, Florida Citrus Commission; pp. 116-117: Bureau of Reclamation, U.S. Air Force Academy, Landwehr-Monkmeyer, Anaconda New Mexico Operations, Dept. of Interior; pp. 118-119: National Film Board, Union Pacific Railroad, Dole, Bureau of Reclamation, American International Pictures, Black Star, De Wys.

13th printing .... **August 1973**

Printed in the U.S.A.

CONTENTS

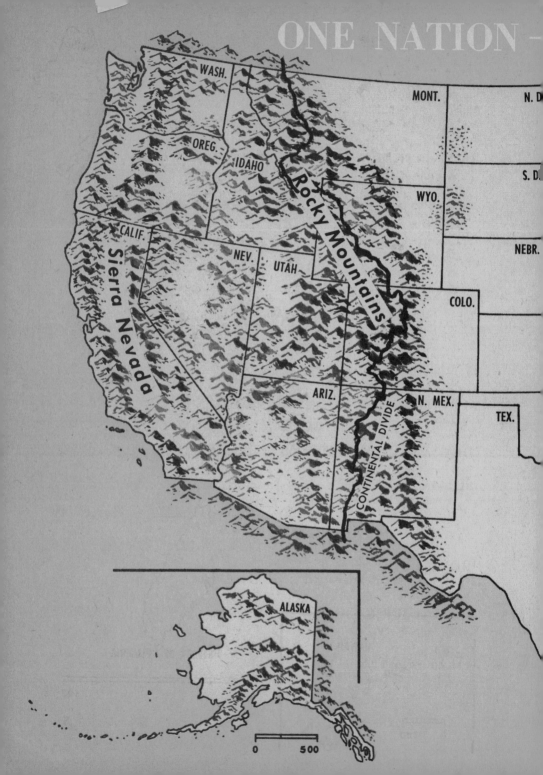

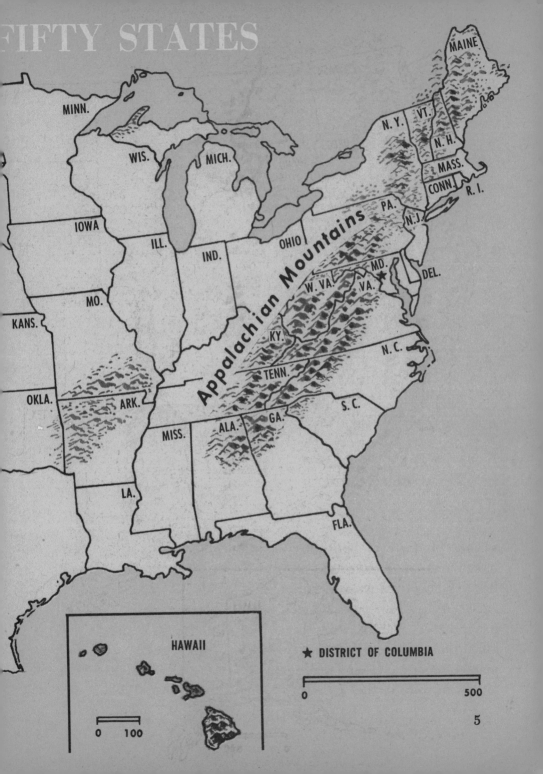

FIFTY STATES

TENNESSEE

Huntsville

TENNESSEE RIVER

Birmingham

MISSISSIPPI

ALABAMA

GEORGIA

TOMBIGBEE RIVER

ALABAMA RIVER

Montgomery

N

Enterprise

Mobile

FLORIDA

GULF OF MEXICO

0   100

• Grateful farmers built this monument at Enterprise. It honors the boll weevil for "what it has done to herald prosperity." When weevils killed their cotton, the farmers planted other crops—and made money in spite of the weevils.

ALABAMA

"The Cotton State" became the 22nd State, 1819

IT was 1910 in Alabama — a terrible year. Boll weevils swarmed in from the west. They chewed their way into the vast cotton fields that covered the state like a snowy blanket. That year, many farmers had nothing to sell. How could they make a living? In time, the farmers learned how to fight the boll weevil. They learned an important lesson as well — not to depend on a single crop. Alabama farmers still make more money from cotton than from any other crop, but they also grow corn, tobacco, peanuts, soybeans, fruit, cattle, and poultry.

In northern Alabama, factories turn Alabama cotton into cloth and cottonseed oil. Where does the power come from that turns the machines? Mainly from the mighty Tennessee River! Its surging waters used to flood homes and farms nearly every year. Today a series of dams prevents flooding and stores the extra water to use when the river is low.

The furnaces of Birmingham blast night and day making iron and steel. The raw materials — iron ore, coal, and limestone — are right in the city's "back yard." Birmingham produces so much steel that it is called the "Pittsburgh of the South."

Pine forests that cover half the state echo to the shouts of loggers and crashing trees. The trees that are cut down are shipped to mills to be made into furniture, pulp, and paper.

Ships come to the port of Mobile to carry Alabama's products to faraway places all over the world.

ALASKA

Became the 49th State, 1959

OUR 49th state is a place of contrasts. Most of Alaska is still a wild frontier, yet you can also find skyscraper apartment houses. An Eskimo puts out to sea in a whaleskin boat, but the boat may be powered by an outboard motor. And a dog team pulls a sled over snow and ice — hurrying to a modern airport.

Alaska is not all snow and ice, however, even in winter. And in summer, the temperature in Fairbanks sometimes soars to 100 degrees. Here truck gardens grow strawberries as big as plums, and the sun — shining until late evening — can give you a good sunburn. The most northerly point in the U.S. is Point Barrow. Here, from May through July, you can fish all night by the light of the midnight sun.

Alaska is BIG — twice as big as Texas. Do you want to climb America's highest mountain? It's in Alaska — Mt. McKinley, 20,320 feet tall. Is there really a glacier as big as Rhode Island? Yes, Malaspina Glacier in southern Alaska. Where is there a volcano with a crater six miles across? This crater, Aniakchak, is near the Valley of Ten Thousand Smokes. Steam and smoke puffing from craters all over this strange valley make it look like some giant's kitchen.

Salmon fishing is the most important industry, but gold is what comes to mind when most people think of Alaska. With the discovery of gold in the late 1800's prospectors poured into Alaska's wilderness. Many of them settled there.

Today Alaska produces more platinum than any other state. Alaskans cut timber for their pulp mills, pump oil from under the sea, and produce many beautiful furs.

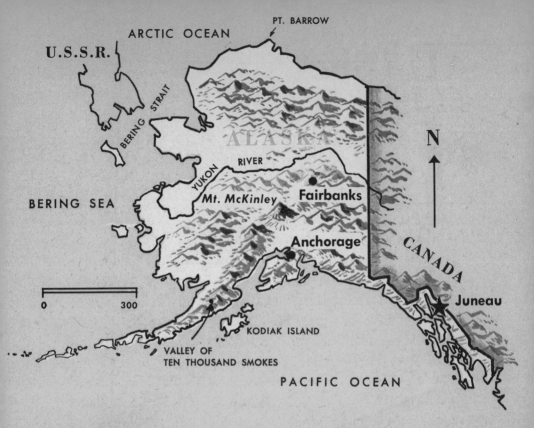

• Huge brown Kodiak bears live on Kodiak Island, south of the Alaska mainland. These bears are the largest of all meat-eating land animals in the world. They may stand ten feet tall and weigh nearly a ton. They enjoy eating salmon, and get their dinner by sweeping the fish out of the streams with their great paws.

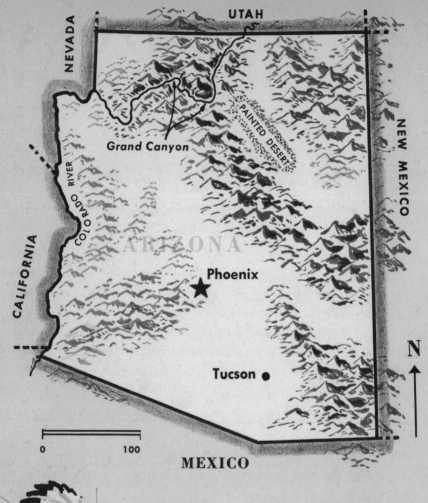

UTAH

NEVADA

NEW MEXICO

Grand Canyon

PAINTED DESERT

COLORADO RIVER

CALIFORNIA

ARIZONA

Phoenix

N

Tucson

0   100

MEXICO

• These Hopi Indians perform the ancient tribal Feather Dance. Hopi Indians still live in the little villages called *pueblos* that their ancestors occupied for hundreds of years.

ARIZONA

"Grand Canyon State" became the 48th State, 1912

 CACTUS, cowboys and Indians. Arizona has them in abundance. A whole *forest* of cactus trees grows near Phoenix. Cowboys? Thousands of them work on ranches. Indians? More Indians live in Arizona than in any other state.

But if some parts of Arizona remind you of a TV western, others take you right into the Atomic Age. Uranium is mined in the hillsides. And in the desert, factories make parts for jets.

Arizona is a land of natural wonders. Its forests and canyons tell exciting stories of the early days of the world. The Grand Canyon is one of the most awesome spectacles on earth. For centuries the Colorado River cut its way through layers of rock. As the river sank, it left red and yellow rock walls *a mile high* on either side. So deep is the Grand Canyon it has different climates at different levels.

The Painted Desert has rainbow-colored sands. Nearby Meteor Crater is a gigantic hole, 600 feet deep and a mile wide. Some scientists think it was made by a huge meteor that crashed millions of years ago. There's a spooky forest in eastern Arizona, too, that was alive centuries ago. Today it is the Petrified Forest, its fallen logs and stunted trees all solid stone.

Arizona is rich in natural resources as well as in natural wonders. About half our nation's copper comes from Arizona's mines. Gold is mined here, as well as lead and silver.

Cotton and citrus fruits grow in Arizona's golden sunshine. And its sunny and dry climate is one reason why the population has doubled since the end of World War II.

11

ARKANSAS

"Land of Opportunity" became the 25th State, 1836

IT was not gold that the Spanish explorer, DeSoto, found in Arkansas, but "magic water." For there are more health-giving mineral springs in Arkansas than anywhere else in the U.S. — 47 of them in Hot Springs National Park. No matter how fiercely the Indians fought one another, they kept Hot Springs as neutral territory which all tribes could use.

Mammoth Spring is one of the largest springs in the world. The two hundred million gallons of water that gush forth from Mammoth each day are stored in two dams and are used to create electric power.

The earth of Arkansas yields more than "magic water." It is rich, too, in minerals, such as bauxite. Nearly all the U.S. output of this important aluminum ore is mined in Arkansas. Along the Arkansas River are vast coal fields. And the only diamond mine in North America is near Murfreesboro. Diamond hunting here is more for fun than for profit. Visitors pay to hunt for diamonds, and they keep what they find.

Forests cover most of the land, but Arkansas is mainly a farming state. In the east are cotton plantations like those in Mississippi. To the southwest, cattle ranches and grazing lands make you think of Texas. And after one look at the bayous, swamps, and moss-hung oaks in southeastern Arkansas, you might guess you were in Louisiana.

The next time you write on the blackboard, think of Chalk Bluff in northeastern Arkansas. This hill contains enough chalk to keep your class supplied for hundreds of years.

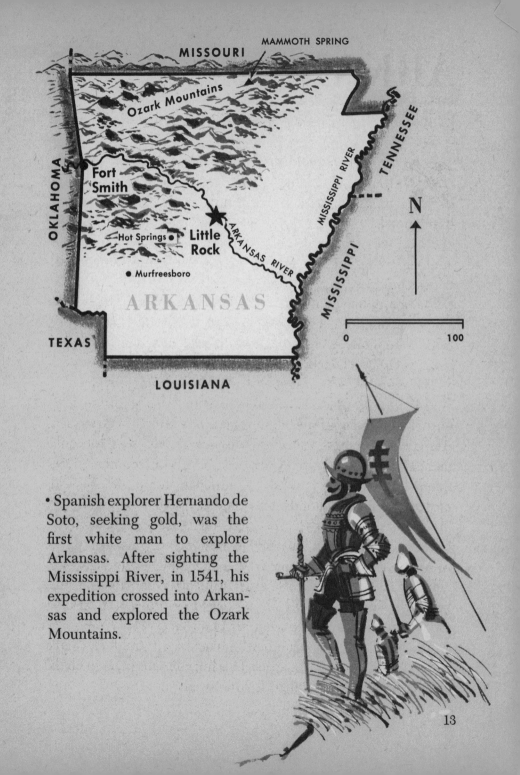

MAMMOTH SPRING

MISSOURI

Ozark Mountains

OKLAHOMA

Fort
Smith

Hot Springs • ★ Little
Rock

• Murfreesboro

ARKANSAS

TEXAS

LOUISIANA

TENNESSEE

MISSISSIPPI RIVER

ARKANSAS RIVER

MISSISSIPPI

N

0   100

• Spanish explorer Hernando de Soto, seeking gold, was the first white man to explore Arkansas. After sighting the Mississippi River, in 1541, his expedition crossed into Arkansas and explored the Ozark Mountains.

13

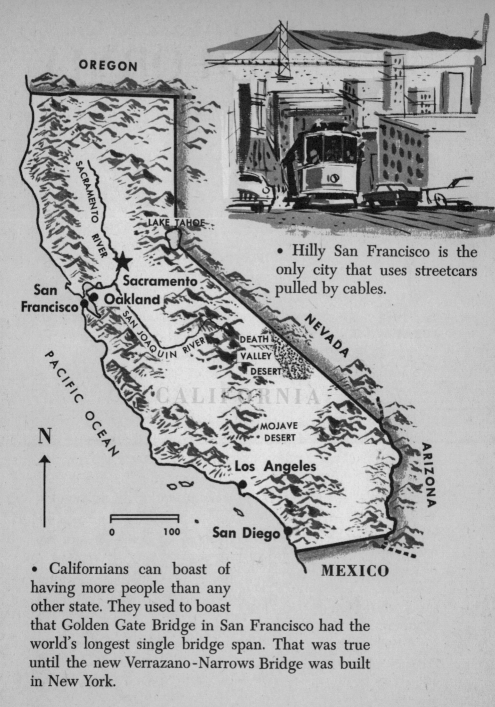

• Hilly San Francisco is the only city that uses streetcars pulled by cables.

• Californians can boast of having more people than any other state. They used to boast that Golden Gate Bridge in San Francisco had the world's longest single bridge span. That was true until the new Verrazano-Narrows Bridge was built in New York.

CALIFORNIA

"The Golden State" became the 31st State, 1850

"EL DORADO — The Golden Place," cried the Spanish explorers in the 1500's.

"Kun Shan — The Golden Hills," murmured Chinese workers, gazing at the hills of San Francisco more than three hundred years later.

"GOLD!" shouted prospectors in 1848, and the famous California Gold Rush began.

There's another kind of gold in California — golden sunshine that helps to grow the greatest fruit and vegetable crops in the U.S. There's "black gold," too — oil bubbling out of the ground from hundreds of oil wells.

California is full of natural wonders. Here is Death Valley, 282 feet below sea level — the lowest land in the U.S. In nearby Sequoia National Park you can see "General Sherman." The General is not a soldier but a sequoia tree, one of the oldest and largest living things in the world.

There's a special kind of stargazing you can do in Los Angeles — watching television stars at work. In Los Angeles, too, are California's "first citizens" — fossils of the Ice Age. They were discovered in the tar pits of La Brea — one of the richest finds of prehistoric fossils ever unearthed. Almost a million years ago, saber-tooth tigers, giant sloths, and other monsters stumbled into the pits, where they were preserved forever in the sticky tar.

Farther north, on the seacoast, is the Vandenberg Air Force Base, where guided missiles and satellites blast off. You travel quickly in California — from Ice Age to Space Age.

COLORADO

"The Centennial State" became the 38th State, 1876

IN 1820, Major Stephen Long, exploring Colorado, called its vast plains the "Great American Desert." He could not know that someday Colorado farms would yield rich crops of wheat, corn, and sugar beets. For today the waters of the Platte and Arkansas rivers irrigate this desert. And water even flows to the land through tunnels in the mountain wall of the Continental Divide.

From a plane, the Continental Divide looks like a giant's backbone. The Divide zigzags north to south through the entire Rocky Mountain Range. Rain falling on the western slope of the Divide flows to the Pacific. Rain falling on the eastern slope ends in the Atlantic Ocean.

This state has half of the highest mountains in the U.S., and once the Colorado Rockies seemed impossible to cross. Today roads wind around the peaks, bridges cross the gorges, trains rush through tunnels blasted into the rock.

On the edge of the mountains at mile-high Denver, gold was discovered in 1858. The next year prospectors thronged to Colorado. This gold rush changed the history of Colorado and made it a state — for towns sprang up and railroads were built. Settlers found not only gold, but other minerals — silver, copper, coal, and oil. Some gave up treasure-hunting and started farms and cattle ranches instead.

Colorado is still a great mining state, and now her hills yield a new kind of treasure — uranium, raw material for atomic energy.

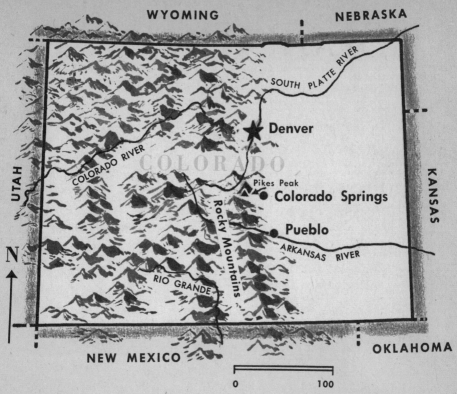

• Pikes Peak is Colorado's most famous mountain. It was named for Zebulon Pike, who discovered it in 1806 and tried to climb it. "Pikes Peak or Bust" became the slogan of gold seekers off to join the Colorado gold rush of 1859. The mountain towers 14,110 feet above sea level.

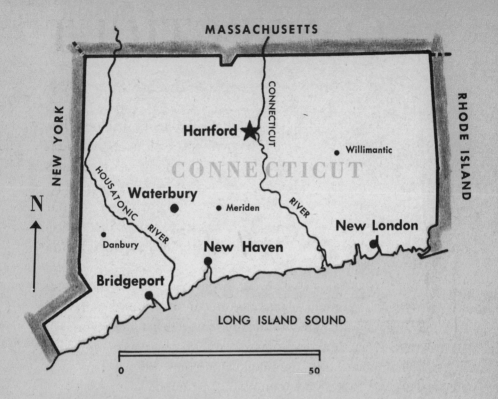

MASSACHUSETTS

NEW YORK

RHODE ISLAND

CONNECTICUT RIVER

Hartford ★

● Willimantic

CONNECTICUT

HOUSATONIC RIVER

N

Waterbury
●

● Meriden

RIVER

New London
●

● Danbury

New Haven
●

Bridgeport
●

LONG ISLAND SOUND

0   50

● Charter Oak was a large tree which once stood in Hartford. It was used as a hiding place in 1687 for Connecticut's charter of self-government. Joseph Wadsworth hid the precious charter in the tree to keep it from being seized by the British governor. Charter Oak blew down in a storm in 1856, but a monument marks the spot where it once stood.

CONNECTICUT

"The Nutmeg State" became the 5th State, 1788

AMERICA's first supersalesmen were Yankee peddlers from Connecticut. They traveled all over the country, their wagons loaded with goods for the homes of pioneer America. Many Connecticut towns still manufacture the same products they made in the early days of our nation. Waterbury is famous for its clocks and brassware, Meriden for its silverware, Willimantic for its thread, and Danbury for its hats.

Connecticut know-how created the wide variety of made-in-Connecticut goods — pins and needles, nuts and bolts and cookbooks. Here Linus Yale manufactured his lock. Here Eli Whitney started modern mass-production by making muskets with machine-made interchangeable parts. Before that, each musket had to be made completely by hand.

"Connecticut" came from the Pequot Indian word for "Long River." The Connecticut River is the longest river in New England. In the valley through which it flows, farmers of Connecticut raise tobacco, potatoes, fruit, and vegetables.

On Long Island Sound, where the "Long River" empties, are the busy ports of Bridgeport, New Haven, and New London. New London is the home of the U.S. Coast Guard Academy. Across the river at Groton Naval Base, the first atomic-powered submarine, the *Nautilus,* was launched.

If you had lived in Abington in 1793, you might have read books from what is now the oldest lending library in the U.S. If you had gone to school at East Haddam in 1774, your teacher might have been — Nathan Hale!

DELAWARE

"The Diamond State" became the 1st State, 1787

 "I SEE a white, sandy shore and an abundance of green trees," Henry Hudson wrote in 1609, as he sailed up the Delaware River.

Imagine that you are taking Hudson for a trip through Delaware today. Instead of trees, Hudson sees abundant smokestacks. Factories are an important part of Wilmington, the state's largest city.

As he sails down the Delaware again, Hudson sees great ocean liners and busy freighters. Piled high on the docks are crates and cartons to be loaded aboard waiting ships.

"These crates hold machinery and ammunition," you say. "And chemicals, dyes, and leather goods. So many chemicals are made here that Wilmington is called the Chemical Capital of the World. And over here are cartons marked 'Nylon.' That's a cloth spun out of coal, air and water."

"Nylon!" exclaims Hudson. " 'Tis more like witchcraft. Does witchcraft make all these wonders?"

"No," you explain. "These goods are made by people."

Hudson holds up a crate of eggs. "These, too?"

You assure him that eggs still come from chickens and that Delaware farms raise millions of them. Then you show him fields of berries, corn, and tomatoes.

Finally you take Henry Hudson to Delaware Bay. You point out the oyster boats with their great derrick-like dredges. "These scoop up the oysters," you say. This is too much! With a deep sigh, the old ghost vanishes from the sandy shores of the state he discovered long ago.

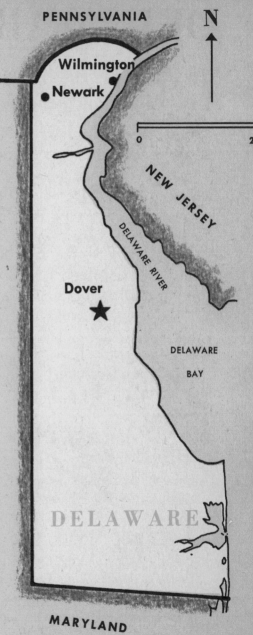

PENNSYLVANIA

N

Wilmington

• Newark

0   20

NEW JERSEY

DELAWARE RIVER

Dover
★

DELAWARE
BAY

DELAWARE

MARYLAND

• Delaware has a special honor. Because it was the first of the thirteen original states to approve the Constitution, Delaware leads the parade of states every four years when the new President is inaugurated.

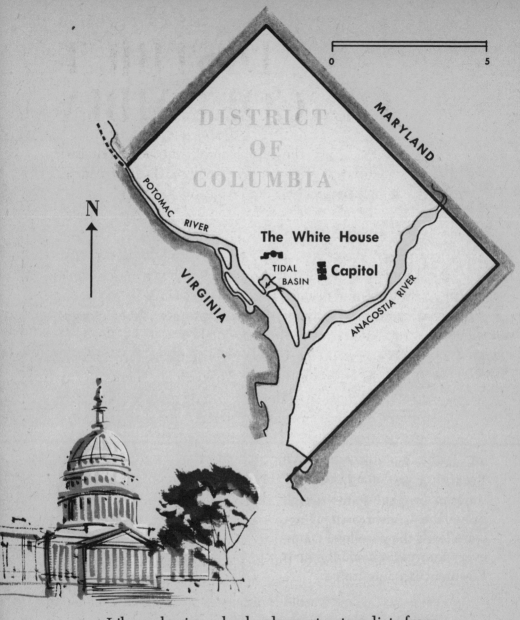

• Like spokes in a wheel, a dozen streets radiate from the Capitol. Here Congress meets to make our country's laws. Washington laid the cornerstone of the Capitol in 1793, and the dome was put on when Lincoln was President. The inauguration of the Presidents takes place on the steps of the Capitol.

DISTRICT OF COLUMBIA

WHICH city is the capital of all our states but isn't a part of any state? Washington, D.C., of course, which became our nation's capital in 1800.

Our first President worked hard to see our capital city built. He chose the site — the banks of the Potomac River. But George Washington never lived in his namesake city. John Adams was the first tenant of the White House, which has been the home of our Presidents ever since.

Government is Washington's main business. Here Congress meets to make our laws. Here the highest court in our land convenes — the Supreme Court. One of every three people in Washington works for the U.S. government. There's plenty of work to be done, too! Here in Washington are the busy "main offices" of government departments such as the Treasury and Agriculture.

The Bureau of Engraving and Printing makes our paper money and stamps. The Library of Congress is one of the world's largest libraries. In the National Archives building, you can see two thrilling original documents — the Declaration of Independence and the Constitution.

Washington is one of the loveliest capitals in the world. It's a city of wide avenues (named for different states), green parks, white marble buildings, and impressive memorials, such as the Jefferson and Lincoln memorials. In the spring Washington is especially beautiful. Then more than 3,000 Japanese cherry trees along the Tidal Basin burst into bloom — a breath-taking sight.

FLORIDA

"The Sunshine State" became the 27th State, 1845

 WHERE do circuses go in the winter? To Sarasota, Florida. Besides circuses in the winter, Florida has hogs that fish and cows that dunk. On Lake George, hogs swim out in the shallow water to catch their fish dinners. The bottom of the lake is covered with thick grass, so cows wade in and dunk their heads underwater to reach their food. At Hialeah Park, near Miami, the pink flamingos eat only with their heads upside down!

Florida has about 30,000 lakes — more than any other state. It also has the longest highway ever built over ocean waters. The Overseas Highway runs from Miami to Key West, spanning the islands called the Florida Keys, at the end of the peninsula of Florida.

Florida tans are famous. Northern visitors acquire them at Florida's sandy beaches and winter resorts.

Florida's jungles are famous, too. In the swampy Everglades deer and panthers roam, and alligators sun themselves.

Where can you eat grapefruit and oranges right from the trees? In Florida, where vegetables and sugar cane are also raised. From Florida's forests comes our main supply of cypress lumber. And from her pine trees comes much of our turpentine. There's cigar making at Tampa, and sponge fishing at nearby Tarpon Springs.

What is the oldest town in the U.S.? St. Augustine, Florida, the first permanent white settlement in the U.S., founded about 1565.

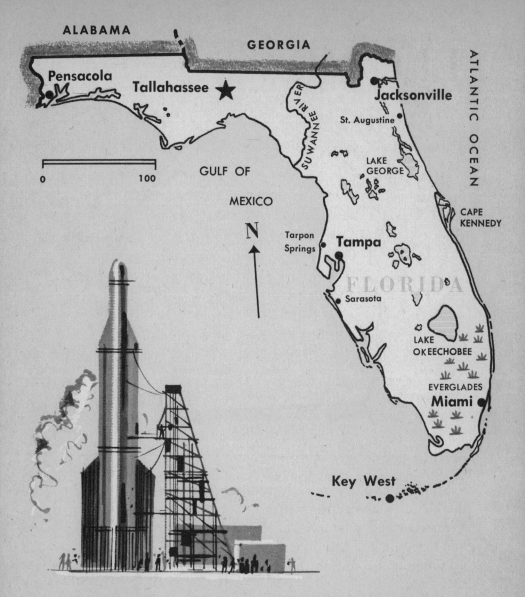

• The John F. Kennedy Space Center is located at Florida's Cape Kennedy. From the cape's launching platforms, huge rockets thunder into space. Explorer I, America's first earth satellite, was launched from Kennedy. So were our first astronauts.

TENNESSEE   NORTH CAROLINA

SOUTH CAROLINA

ALABAMA

CHATTAHOOCHEE RIVER

SAVANNAH RIVER

★ Atlanta

• Warm Springs

N ↑

● Columbus

GEORGIA

Savannah

SEA ISLANDS

OKEFENOKEE SWAMP

ATLANTIC OCEAN

FLORIDA

0   100

• Franklin D. Roosevelt, thirty-second President of the U.S.A., was stricken with polio at the age of 39. Treatment and swimming at Warm Springs helped him to regain much of his strength. To help other polio sufferers, he started the Warm Springs Foundation.

GEORGIA

"Empire State of the South" became the 4th State, 1788

 THE climate was perfect for raising cotton. Georgia's farmers knew it. But few of them wanted the weary job of separating cotton fiber from its seed. Then in 1793, in Savannah, Eli Whitney invented his cotton gin — a mechanical wonder that could clean the seeds from 350 pounds of cotton in one day! Cotton became king in Georgia — her main crop for many years. And soon there were textile mills busily turning the cotton into cloth.

Cotton is still an important crop, and Georgia is the third largest producer of cotton goods in the U.S. Her farmers also grow pecans, watermelons, tobacco, corn, the famous Georgia peaches — and peanuts. More peanuts are grown in Georgia than in any other state.

The newsprint for some of your newspapers and the plastics for some of your games may have begun life in the pine forests which cover two thirds of Georgia. From Georgia's quarries came the marble stone for the beautiful Lincoln Memorial in Washington, D.C.

Georgia is the biggest state east of the Mississippi River. With a coastline almost 100 miles long and Appalachian peaks rising in the north, her scenery is richly varied. Just off the shore are the famous Sea Islands. And in the south is vast, eerie Okefenokee Swamp, "the place of trembling earth," where floating islands of tangled weeds tremble under the slightest weight. Okefenokee is one of the largest swamps in the U.S. Much of Okefenokee is still a mysterious place that has never been explored.

HAWAII

"The Aloha State" became the 50th State, 1959

THE HAWAIIAN word *Aloha* means several things — "welcome," "good-by," "love," and "friendship." It also seems to describe the way people from many parts of the world live together on these beautiful islands in peace and friendship. A Hawaiian-American boy or girl may have ancestors from such faraway places as Japan, China, Europe, North America, or the Philippine Islands.

Our newest state is our only island state. It is really a chain of 20 islands, formed by the tops of undersea mountains. Most of these are so small they are just dots on a map. People live only on the seven largest islands.

Oahu is the most important island because of Honolulu, Hawaii's capital, biggest port, and only large city. Here, too, is our great naval base, Pearl Harbor.

Hawaii grows more sugar cane than any other state, and much of it comes from Kauai, the "Garden Island." Near Kauai's highest point is Mount Waialeale, one of the world's rainiest places.

Lanai is a big pineapple plantation. From the Hawaiian Islands come most of the world's canned pineapple products.

On Maui there is an immense sleeping volcano. Once, in a fiery explosion, it blew its top off. The hole that was left is the world's largest inactive-volcano crater.

The giant volcanoes of Mauna Kea and Mauna Loa rise over "Big Island," Hawaii, which has the same name as the state. Here you can see cowboys herding cattle on big ranches.

Hawaiians greet their thousands of visitors with garlands of flowers called *leis*, and the friendly cry, *"Aloha!"*

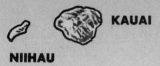

KAUAI

NIIHAU

0   100

OAHU

Honolulu

PACIFIC OCEAN

MOLOKAI

MAUI

N

HAWAII

LANAI

KAHOOLAWE

• Surfboard riding over the waves is a popular sport among Hawaiian children and grownups. It was invented long ago by the kings and chieftains of Hawaii. Surfboarding requires skill and courage but it comes easily to our island-dwelling citizens.

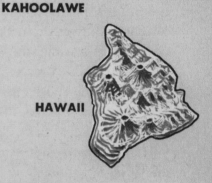

HAWAII

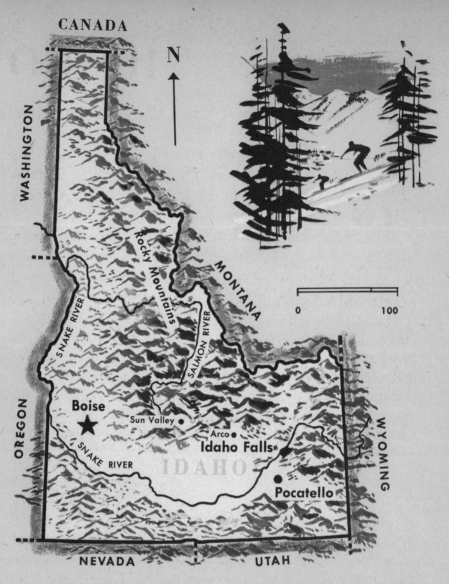

• Vacationers from all over the world come to Sun Valley's famous sports resort. During the winter visitors can enjoy skiing on Sun Valley's twenty ski runs. In the summer tourists can hunt, fish, or go mountain climbing. Sun Valley is 6,000 feet above sea level and is encircled by snowy peaks.

IDAHO

"The Gem State" became the 43rd State, 1890

 IF you woke up one morning in a park near Sun Valley called Craters of the Moon, you might think you *were* on the moon. You would see brightly colored lava fields and the dead craters of extinct volcanoes.

Other things in Idaho seem to come out of science fiction, too. There are caves whose walls are thick with ice that never melts. Other caves contain springs so hot that the water is piped out to heat homes.

In the Snake River live giant white sturgeon, the biggest fresh-water fish in North America. Some weigh more than a thousand pounds. In order to pull out a big one, fishermen have been known to hitch their lines to a two-horse wagon.

Most people in Idaho live on or near the banks of the Snake. From this river's surging waters comes their electrical power. The Snake is certainly not "small potatoes"!

In fact, Idaho boasts that it doesn't have any small potatoes — only the big Idaho potatoes that grow in the farmlands of the Snake River plains.

The jagged mountains of Idaho's Rockies are as fierce as their names — Sawtooth, Seven Devils, Bitterroot. There are riches in the Idaho mountains — gold and zinc, antimony, cobalt and lead, and semi-precious stones. The largest silver mines in the U.S. are in Idaho, too.

Near the edge of the mountains not far from Sun Valley, is an important center for atomic research. Here, at Arco, the first electricity ever to come from atomic energy was produced in 1951.

ILLINOIS

"The Prairie State" became the 21st State, 1818

DOWN the Illinois River the early settlers sailed. Down the Ohio, the Wabash, and the Mississippi, too. They came to Illinois by keelboat and barge, and they came overland by wagon.

Some came to farm the fertile meadows. And as Illinois farmers do even today, they raised corn, hogs, and cattle and shipped them to market down their river highways. Some settlers came to build and work in towns. Thus the cities of Rockford, Decatur, Joliet, and Peoria grew. Still others came to mine the coal needed for the growing factories. Today these factories produce the most farm machinery, candy, and corn products in the nation.

In the late 1700's, one man came to Illinois from the far-away island of Haiti. He was Jean Baptiste Point du Sable, a Negro freedman. The trading post he built on the shores of Lake Michigan was the beginning of a mighty city — Chicago!

Today Chicago leads the world as a railway center and as a grain and livestock market. It's our largest lake port, and second only to New York City in printing and publishing.

Chicago and its neighbor cities produce more steel than Pittsburgh. Raw materials, such as the iron ore from mines near Lake Superior, are transported easily and cheaply to the foundries and steel mills of Chicago and its suburbs and, just across the state line, Gary, Indiana.

In 1871 the Great Chicago Fire destroyed almost the entire city. What started the fire? Mrs. O'Leary's cow, they say, kicked over a kerosene lamp.

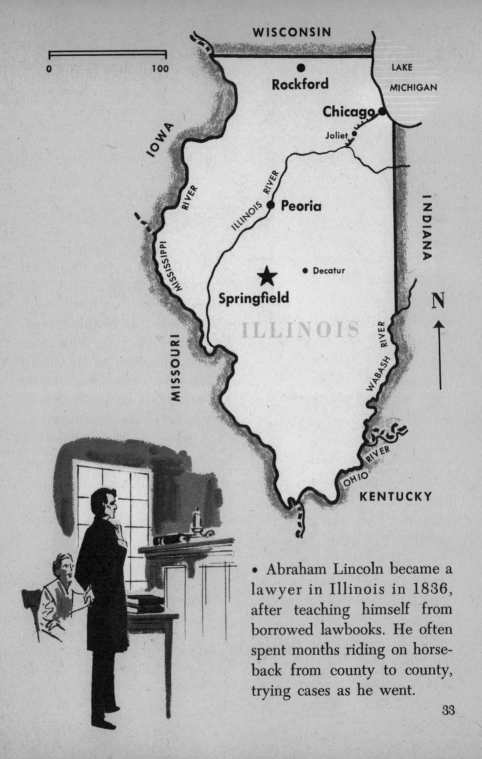

WISCONSIN

0   100

IOWA

Rockford

LAKE MICHIGAN

Chicago

Joliet

MISSISSIPPI RIVER

ILLINOIS RIVER

Peoria

INDIANA

Decatur

★ Springfield

ILLINOIS

N

MISSOURI

WABASH RIVER

OHIO RIVER

KENTUCKY

• Abraham Lincoln became a lawyer in Illinois in 1836, after teaching himself from borrowed lawbooks. He often spent months riding on horseback from county to county, trying cases as he went.

33

N

• During the Revolutionary War, the American troops led by George Rogers Clark captured Vincennes, a fortified village held by British troops. Clark's victory at Vincennes made it possible for the United States to claim boundaries westward as far as the Mississippi River and northward all the way to the Great Lakes.

INDIANA

"The Hoosier State" became the 19th State, 1816

HOW fast can a city grow? At first there were just empty sand dunes where Gary, Indiana, stands today. In 1905, a steel company bought the dunes and built Gary. Ever since, Gary has been an important, busy, steel-making city. It's right on Lake Michigan, so boats can bring in iron ore. Railroads bring in the coal and carry the finished products to the nation.

Indianapolis, largest city in Indiana, was also "made to order." Indiana's people decided to have their capital right in the center of the state, so they built Indianapolis in the middle of a dense forest.

Indiana has busy farms as well as bustling cities. It is one of the leading states in growing corn and soybeans — and hogs, too. On its level plains, the farmers raise hay, rye, oats, vegetables, and tobacco, and its fields of wheat stretch to the horizon like a golden sea. When the grain is cut, the stacks look like yellow wigwams.

Real wigwams once dotted the plains of Indiana, for this was the home of the Shawnee and Miami Indians.

Only a few miles apart, in southern Indiana, are two unusual places. One of the world's largest caves is near Wyandotte, where narrow passages wind for miles through underground rooms.

The other special place is a town named Santa Claus. Many letters addressed to Santa find their way here. Who answers them? The good-hearted people of the town!

IOWA

 MOST of Iowa is a king-size prairie, almost as flat as the floor in your room. And on this land grows a living carpet of grain and hay. Iowa's farmers raise so many crops, cattle, and hogs that its people say: "Iowa feeds the nation."

Iowa has always been good farmland. Before white men came, Indians raised corn, tilling their fields with pointed deerhorns. How astonished these Indians would be if they could see Iowa today! Modern farm machinery, made in Iowa's cities, helps turn the soil and harvest the crops.

The Indians would marvel, too, at the up-to-date meat-packing plants which turn Iowa livestock into pork, beef, and mutton. But they would see one familiar sight. In Muscatine, factories make "pearl" buttons from shells of mussels. These come from the Mississippi and other nearby rivers, and are the same kind of shells that Indians used to make necklaces and spoons.

Iowans can boast of more than their king-size prairies that grow king-size corn. They also have the largest washing machine factory, the largest cereal mill, and the largest popcorn processing plant in the U.S.

One of Iowa's proudest boasts is its leadership in education. No other state has a better record in teaching its people to read and write.

The town of Pella was founded in 1847 by settlers from the Netherlands. Now every May, Pella holds a Dutch Tulip Festival. The town dresses up in tulips and the townsfolk dress up in wooden shoes.

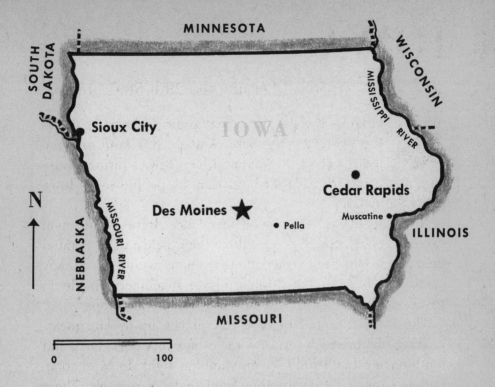

• Iowa has some of the richest soil in the world and takes turns with Illinois in growing the most corn of any state. Some of the corn is made into corn meal and cereal, but most of it goes to feed hogs and cattle.

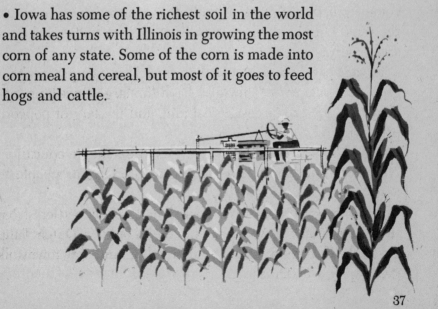

37

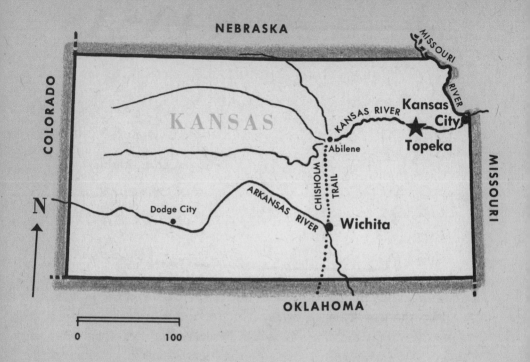

NEBRASKA

MISSOURI RIVER

COLORADO

KANSAS

KANSAS RIVER

Kansas City

Abilene

CHISHOLM TRAIL

Topeka

MISSOURI

N

Dodge City

ARKANSAS RIVER

Wichita

OKLAHOMA

0   100

• William Frederick Cody got his nickname of "Buffalo Bill" by shooting thousands of buffalo to provide meat for the hungry men who built the Kansas Pacific Railroad. Cody had been a Pony Express rider and served as an Army scout. He also organized America's first Wild West Show, which featured cowboys and Indians, performing daredevil feats of riding, roping, and shooting.

KANSAS

"The Sunflower State" became the 34th State, 1861

THE Spanish explorer Coronado came to Kansas in 1541, looking for gold. Instead, he found Indian villages and miles and miles of flat land.

Today he would see gold in Kansas — vast golden fields of wheat and corn edged with the gold of sunflowers. Kansas grows so much winter wheat and makes so much flour that the state is nicknamed the "breadbasket of the nation."

Much of the wheat goes to Kansas City and Wichita, which have the largest flour mills. Here, too, are stockyards and meat-packing plants, oil fields, and airplane factories.

Two pioneer Kansas towns, Abilene and Dodge City, are famous in song and story. In the 1870's they were wild frontier towns. Weary cowboys drove herds of cattle to market along the Chisholm Trail from Texas to Abilene. On the streets of Dodge City, desperados shot it out with strong-nerved sheriffs and marshals. Here Bat Masterson and Wyatt Earp served terms as peace officers.

Kansas towns are no longer wild, but Kansas weather is still untamed. The wind blows and blows and once in a while it blows up a rip-roaring tornado. (It was a Kansas storm that blew Dorothy to the Land of Oz!)

Before the Civil War, this state was known as "Bleeding Kansas," because so many battles were fought here over slavery. Some people wanted Kansas to be a free state. Others wanted to keep slaves. Kansas remained loyal to the Union, and one fifth of her men fought against slavery as soldiers in the Civil War.

KENTUCKY

"The Blue Grass State" became the 15th State, 1792

 KENTUCKY was our first state west of the Appalachian Mountains. It took brave men and women to settle this frontier — pioneers like those Daniel Boone led through the Cumberland Gap in 1775. Encircled by hostile Indians, they built their fort, called it Boonesboro — and *stayed*.

Many Indian battles were fought in Kentucky, and it came to be known as the *dark and bloody ground*. But when the Indian wars were over, the settlers found Kentucky a good place to live in. They liked the mild climate and the fine rich soil.

Today in this fertile soil Kentucky farmers grow the nation's second largest tobacco crop. Once, tobacco was the only crop. It was even used instead of money. Now vegetables, fruit, and grain also grow here. And grass seed from the farms of Kentucky has sprouted in parks and lawns in many parts of the world. Kentucky's horse farms are famous, too, for the fine race horses they breed.

Kentucky has rich coal deposits and ranks second as a coal-producing state. She also takes from her earth oil and gas, clay and limestone. There's gold underground in Kentucky but it won't ever start a gold rush. For this treasure is America's gold reserve, and our government keeps it stored in underground vaults at Fort Knox.

Kentucky has another kind of under-the-earth "treasure" in Mammoth Cave. Imagine a cave with rooms high enough to hold a twelve-story building, with lakes and waterfalls and rushing rivers — a vast underground world!

40

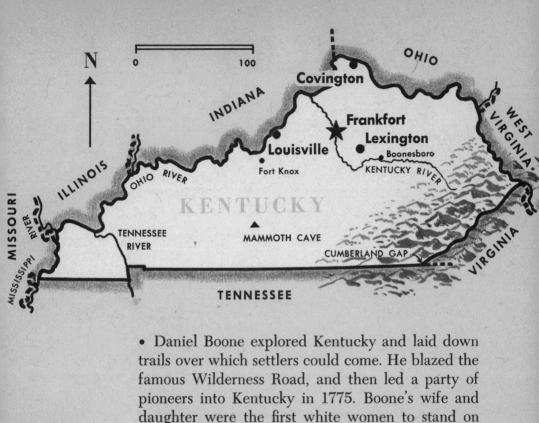

• Daniel Boone explored Kentucky and laid down trails over which settlers could come. He blazed the famous Wilderness Road, and then led a party of pioneers into Kentucky in 1775. Boone's wife and daughter were the first white women to stand on the banks of the Kentucky River.

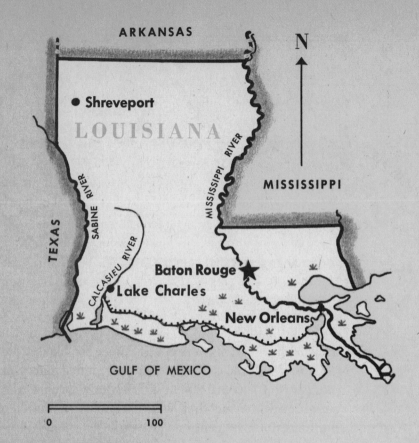

ARKANSAS

N

● Shreveport

LOUISIANA

SABINE RIVER

MISSISSIPPI RIVER

MISSISSIPPI

TEXAS

CALCASIEU RIVER

Baton Rouge ★

● Lake Charles

New Orleans

GULF OF MEXICO

0   100

• New Orleans' Mardi Gras carnival takes place every year just before Lent. This festival was introduced by French colonists long ago. During Mardi Gras, parades, floats, and masks bob up everywhere. The name Mardi Gras means "fat Tuesday" in French — a time for feasting and fun.

LOUISIANA

"The Pelican State" became the 18th State, 1812

FROM frogs to fish, Louisiana is a land of "mosts." It grows more sugar cane than any state but Hawaii. More muskrats are trapped in its swamps than in our other states and Canada combined. One of the biggest catches of fish is taken by Louisiana fishermen from the Gulf of Mexico. There *are* more frogs in Louisiana than in any other state. And the greatest variety of game birds in the U.S. can be found here, many of them living in large sanctuaries where wildlife is protected.

Louisiana's main cities are deep-water ports — New Orleans, Lake Charles, and the capital city of Baton Rouge. The state's largest city is New Orleans, one of the nation's major ports. About a hundred years ago steamboats carried goods and passengers up the Mississippi to St. Louis in Missouri. Today ships sail from New Orleans with cotton, sugar, and oil for ports in both nearby and faraway lands.

The United States government bought the Louisiana Territory from France in 1803 for fifteen million dollars. Louisiana was one of thirteen new states or parts of states that were formed from this territory.

The French influence is still so strong that New Orleans has been called the "Paris of America." The Old French Quarter in the city, the Vieux Carre, is known for its restaurants and shops. New Orleans is also famous for the gayest festival in the South — the Mardi Gras. People wear wonderful costumes and hold colorful parades and pageants. Even the lampposts of New Orleans dress up for the Mardi Gras!

MAINE

"The Pine Tree State" became the 23rd State, 1820

WHERE does the sun rise first in the U.S.A.? In Eastport, Maine – most easterly city in America.

Where do Florida fish go for their vacation? Some end up in Maine's Kennebec River. Great tides from the Atlantic Ocean sweep into the Kennebec, bringing in all kinds of fish from the sea.

The lumbering industry of America was born in Maine. In colonial days, when Maine was a part of the Massachusetts Bay Colony, the British Navy ordered all Maine pines over two feet thick to be marked "Reserved." These great trees became the booms and masts of England's sailing ships.

The first American-made ship was built in Maine, and shipbuilding continued to be an important industry for years. Today trees of Maine provide the pulp out of which paper is made in Maine's paper mills. Her factories also turn out shoes and textiles.

Many a mouth-watering meal travels to your dinner table from Maine. Big lobsters, potatoes, and blueberry pie, for example! Maine catches three fourths of the nation's lobsters. It grows more potatoes than any other state except Idaho and more blueberries than any other state except Michigan.

Would you like to explore the green forests of our largest New England state? Or paddle in a canoe down her rivers and streams? Or see Maine's highest mountain — Mount Katahdin? You won't find a better guide than one of Maine's own Indians. They are very much in demand, for Maine and vacations go together like ham and eggs.

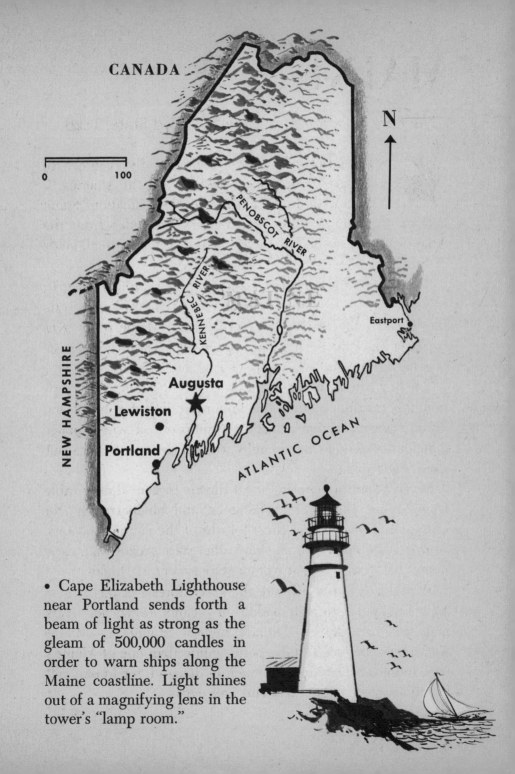

CANADA

N

0   100

PENOBSCOT RIVER

KENNEBEC RIVER

NEW HAMPSHIRE

Eastport

Augusta

Lewiston

Portland

ATLANTIC OCEAN

• Cape Elizabeth Lighthouse
near Portland sends forth a
beam of light as strong as the
gleam of 500,000 candles in
order to warn ships along the
Maine coastline. Light shines
out of a magnifying lens in the
tower's "lamp room."

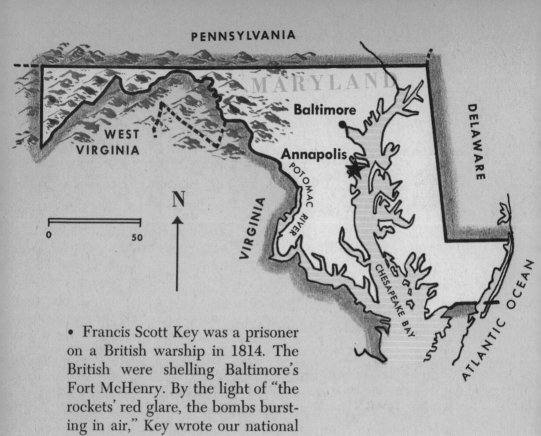

PENNSYLVANIA

MARYLAND

WEST VIRGINIA

Baltimore

Annapolis

DELAWARE

VIRGINIA

POTOMAC RIVER

CHESAPEAKE BAY

ATLANTIC OCEAN

N

0   50

• Francis Scott Key was a prisoner on a British warship in 1814. The British were shelling Baltimore's Fort McHenry. By the light of "the rockets' red glare, the bombs bursting in air," Key wrote our national anthem, "The Star-Spangled Banner."

MARYLAND

"The Old Line State" became the 7th State, 1788

 MARYLAND has an open doorway to the sea — Chesapeake Bay. On the map, the Bay looks like a ragged tear that divides Maryland in two.

From Chesapeake Bay and its jagged inlets, Maryland fishermen haul in millions of pounds of fish, oysters, crabs, and clams each year. On the Eastern Shore are the truck farms where corn, wheat, and tomatoes are raised. Maryland's fruit and vegetable crop is canned or frozen on the Eastern Shore or sent fresh to large eastern cities.

Because Chesapeake Bay is big and deep enough for ocean-going ships, Baltimore is a great port city. In colonial days, it was the furthest inland of all U.S. ports and a gateway to the West. The rich coal fields of Maryland's neighbor states made Baltimore a great coal-shipping center. Today her steel and shipbuilding plants make Baltimore a major industrial city as well.

Maryland's capital, Annapolis, was once the capital of the U.S. From 1783 to 1784 Congress met in the State House. Annapolis is also the home of the U.S. Naval Academy. In the chapel of the Academy lies the body of America's first great naval hero — John Paul Jones.

The next time you travel on a train, think of Maryland, where the first passenger-carrying American railway was built. Maryland saw another important beginning, too. In 1844, in Washington, D. C., Samuel F. B. Morse tapped out a message on his new invention. To Baltimore came those historic first words ever sent by telegraph: WHAT HATH GOD WROUGHT?

MASSACHUSETTS

"The Bay State" became the 6th State, 1788

 WALKING in and around Boston is like strolling through American history. You are not far from the very ground where the Battle of Bunker Hill was fought. In the Old State House, you see a bottle of tea that came from the Boston Tea Party. And you look up at the belfry of the Old North Church, half expecting to see the two lanterns that told Paul Revere the British were coming by sea.

The first library, the first newspaper, the first public school, the first college in America — they all began in Massachusetts. And in 1621 the Pilgrims celebrated the first Thanksgiving.

The cranberries you eat at *your* Thanksgiving dinner may have come from Massachusetts too — from the bogs on Cape Cod. Massachusetts grows more cranberries than any other state.

Today in Massachusetts the valley of the Connecticut River yields harvests of hay, tobacco, and vegetables. But the first colonists had a hard time raising crops on the stony ground where they settled. Later they turned to manufacturing. The first successful U.S. iron works was built in Massachusetts. Today Massachusetts makes much of our cotton fabric and most of our shoes. Its electronics industry is growing fast.

Back in the 1800's Massachusetts boys seeking adventure signed up on the whaling boats that sailed out of New Bedford, Salem, and Nantucket. Whale-hunting was a big business then. So was the building of Boston's fast "Yankee Clipper" sailing ships. The clipper ships are gone, but there are still wind-filled sails in the coves and bays of Massachusetts. For in this state sailing is a favorite sport.

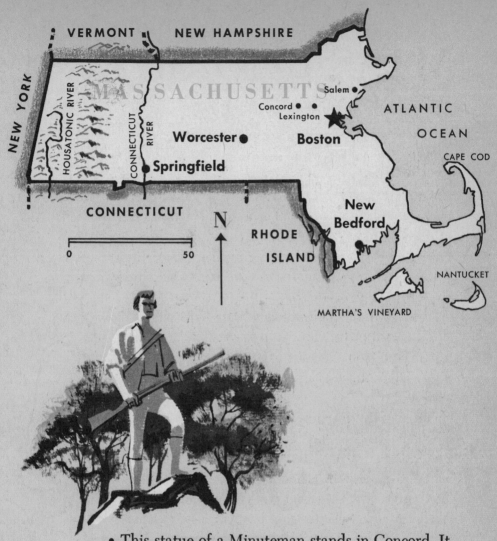

• This statue of a Minuteman stands in Concord. It is dedicated to the memory of the men who volunteered to bear arms "at a minute's notice" to defend their country during the Revolutionary War. Massachusetts Minutemen fought bravely against British troops in the battles of Concord and Lexington. The "shot heard round the world," which began the war, was fired at Lexington on April 19, 1775.

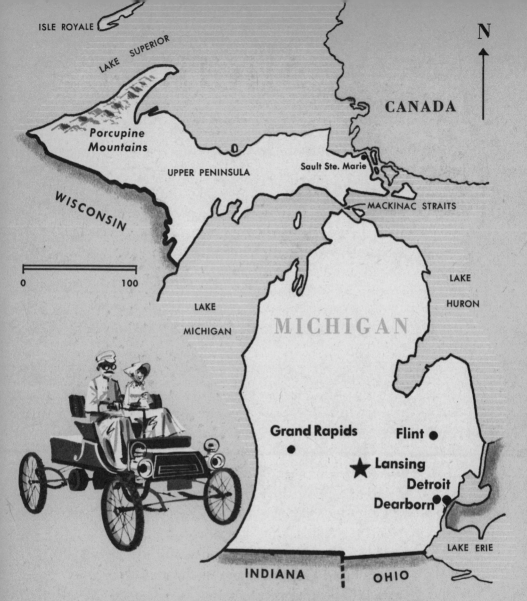

ISLE ROYALE

LAKE SUPERIOR

CANADA

N

Porcupine
Mountains

UPPER PENINSULA

Sault Ste. Marie

WISCONSIN

MACKINAC STRAITS

0   100

LAKE
HURON

LAKE

MICHIGAN

MICHIGAN

Grand Rapids

Flint ●

★ Lansing

Detroit

Dearborn ●

LAKE ERIE

INDIANA   OHIO

● The mass production of autos began in Detroit
when a man named Ransom Olds began building a
car called the Oldsmobile. Then Henry Ford speed-
ed up production with conveyor belts and assembly
lines. This cut the time it took to assemble a car from
14 hours to 93 minutes. Now it takes about an hour.

MICHIGAN

"The Wolverine State" became the 26th State, 1837

 DETROIT, Michigan's largest city, has been called the world's Car Capital. More autos are made in and around Detroit than in any other place. And although it is 1,600 miles from the ocean, Detroit is one of the nation's largest ports. Thanks to the St. Lawrence Seaway, ocean vessels can now sail from the Atlantic to the Great Lakes — right to the docks of Detroit.

Michigan is the only state whose shores are washed by four of the five Great Lakes. There's almost as much traffic on Michigan's waterways as on her city streets. The Sault Sainte Marie Canal carries more freight than any other canal in the world. Barges sail through with iron ore to be made into steel that will be made into cars. The iron comes partly from Minnesota, partly from the rich mines of Michigan's own Upper Peninsula.

From the lonely pine woods of the Upper Peninsula, you can drive across Mackinac Straits on mighty Mackinac Bridge, one of the world's longest suspension bridges.

Go south along Lake Michigan and you're in a fruit belt where more cherries grow than anywhere else in America. Chilly lake winds keep buds from opening till spring frosts are past. The winds also blow fall frosts away till the fruit is ripe.

In the modern city of Dearborn there's an early-American village — Greenfield Village, created by Henry Ford, pioneer auto maker. Here you can go right back into yesterday and see an old mill, a cigar-store Indian, a river boat — even a reproduction of Thomas Edison's first laboratory.

MINNESOTA

MILLIONS of years ago in Minnesota, great glaciers moved across the land. They scooped out thousands of hollows. As the glaciers melted, the hollows filled with water to become Minnesota's sky-blue lakes.

As the glaciers pushed like bulldozers across the rocky ridges of northeast Minnesota, most of the soil was stripped away. This left the world's richest iron-ore deposit so close to the surface that power shovels could scoop up the ore. The shovels have dug so deep that, at Hibbing, they've made the largest man-made hole in the world. From this open-pit mine and others nearby, comes half of our nation's iron ore. This ore is loaded on cargo boats at the port city of Duluth. Then it goes east across Lake Superior, world's largest fresh-water lake, to the great steel mills.

With so much iron ore in Minnesota, you might think mining was the largest industry. Yet Minnesota is chiefly a food-producing state — often called our "Bread and Butter State." Vast quantities of flour for making bread are milled in Minnesota's towns, and only Wisconsin produces more butter.

Minnesota has its own Tale of Two Cities. These are the twin cities that face each other on opposite sides of the Mississippi — St. Paul, capital of the state, and Minneapolis, its largest city.

Some like it hot. Some like it cold. In Minnesota you're lucky if you like both. For in winter the temperature may dip more than 40 degrees below zero, and in summer it may zoom above 100 degrees.

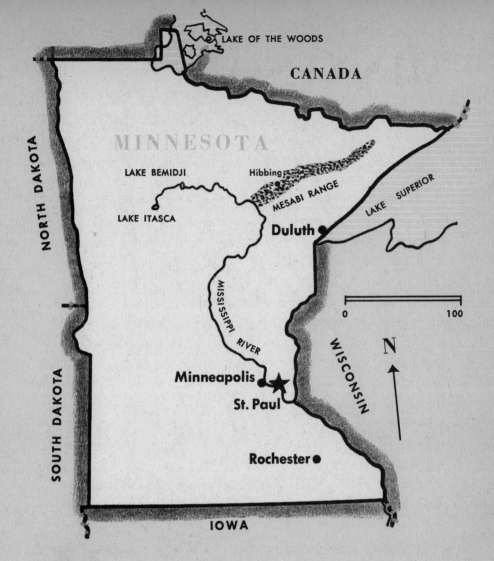

LAKE OF THE WOODS

CANADA

MINNESOTA

NORTH DAKOTA

LAKE BEMIDJI

Hibbing

MESABI RANGE

LAKE SUPERIOR

LAKE ITASCA

Duluth

MISSISSIPPI RIVER

WISCONSIN

0   100

N

Minneapolis

St. Paul

SOUTH DAKOTA

Rochester

IOWA

• Paul Bunyan is a favorite hero of American folklore. He was a giant lumberjack, "as strong as a hundred men." His friend and companion was Babe — the immense Blue Ox, who drank rivers dry. These statues stand by Lake Bemidji.

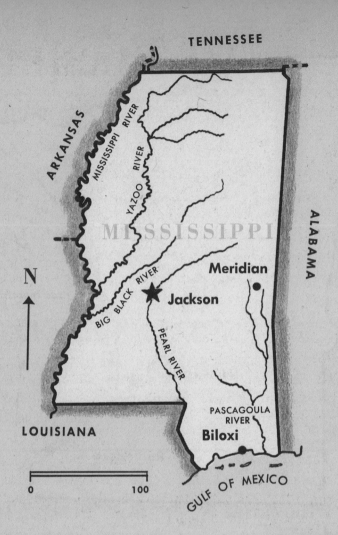

TENNESSEE

ARKANSAS

MISSISSIPPI RIVER

YAZOO RIVER

MISSISSIPPI

ALABAMA

N

BIG BLACK RIVER

Meridian

Jackson

PEARL RIVER

PASCAGOULA RIVER

Biloxi

LOUISIANA

0   100

GULF OF MEXICO

• Captains of steamboats on the Mississippi River were proud of their vessels' speed, and often held races. In the last and most famous race, in 1870, the *Robert E. Lee* beat the *Natchez* from New Orleans to St. Louis.

MISSISSIPPI

"The Magnolia State" became the 20th State, 1817

MISSISSIPPI is a land of farms. The warm wet climate and rich black soil make it easy to raise peanuts, soybeans, sugar, corn, and rice. And cotton, of course! This sunny state ranks third as a cotton producer. The dairy farmers of Mississippi are busy, too. They feed and milk more than two million cows every day.

Mississippi sends what she produces far and wide. How do her goods travel? Down the greatest river highway in the land — the Mississippi River. From the wharves of any Mississippi river town, you can see cargoes of corn and cotton being loaded onto boats and barges.

Lumber is an important cargo, too, for Mississippi is a land of forests as well as rivers. Forests cover more than half the state. Cutting down trees is one way of earning a living here. Working in the sawmills that turn logs into lumber is another. Oil production is also important in Mississippi today.

When the river rises higher than its banks, the friendly Mississippi becomes an enemy. Artificial river banks called levees have been built to keep the rising waters from washing away homes and farms.

Other long rivers with lively names wind through the Magnolia State. Stretching out like two arms from the Mississippi River flow the Big Black and Yazoo rivers. Off to the Gulf of Mexico wander the waters of the Pascagoula and Pearl rivers. A boat trip down the Pearl will take you past cypress swamps, bayous, and Jackson, Mississippi's capital and largest city.

MISSOURI

"The Show Me State" became the 24th State, 1821

 "WANTED — young, skinny, wiry fellows not over 18. Must be expert riders, willing to risk death daily. Orphans preferred. Wages $25 a week."

This ad appeared in a Missouri newspaper in 1860. The daring boys who got the jobs became riders for the Pony Express. They carried the mail from St. Joseph, Missouri, to San Francisco, California, riding through howling snow storms and burning deserts. Indians chased them and bandits shot at them. But the Pony Express Riders got the mail through in ten days.

St. Louis, Missouri's largest city, was once a small trading post for fur trappers. Today this great port on the Mississippi River is a city of skyscrapers and bustling wharves. Beverages, chemicals, drugs, and shoes are produced in its factories. Missouri's second largest city, Kansas City, is a great livestock and wheat market.

North of the Missouri River and in the southeast, the soil is fertile and black, yielding a rich harvest of cotton, corn and wheat. So varied are Missouri's resources that this state also mines more lead and raises more mules than any other.

The Ozark Mountains of southern Missouri are rich in springs and caves to explore. The Indians believed these caves were doorways to a life after death.

Which state lies halfway between the Atlantic and the Rocky Mountains? And halfway between Canada and the Gulf of Mexico? Missouri — crossroads of the continental United States.

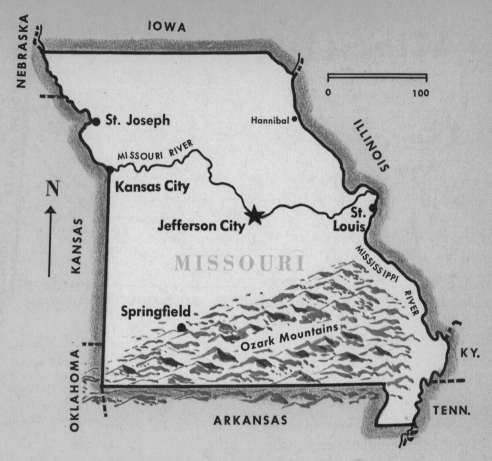

• This statue of Tom Sawyer and Huck Finn stands in Hannibal, a monument to the adventurous boys author Mark Twain wrote about. Twain's boyhood home in Hannibal is now a museum. Beside the house stands a fence like the one Tom Sawyer tricked his friends into whitewashing for him.

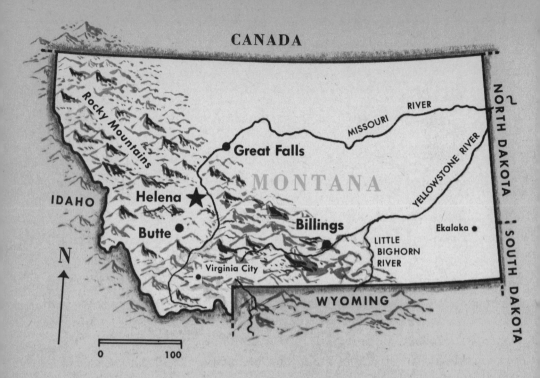

• Montana's forests cover more than 22 million acres, about one fourth of the state. U.S. Forest Rangers keep a sky-high lookout for dangerous forest fires by patrolling the area in helicopters.

MONTANA

"The Treasure State" became the 41st State, 1889

 LESS than a hundred years ago, Montana was the Wild West. Great buffalo herds grazed the plains. Prospectors panned eagerly for gold at Last Chance Gulch and Virginia City. Indians and white men fought for the land, and at Little Bighorn River, General Custer and his men were killed by the Sioux Indians.

Montana has changed. Cattle, sheep, and horses graze where buffalo once roamed. Wheat, barley, and sugar beets are now grown where Indian battles were fought, and oil is a major source of income. There are cities where food and wood products are processed. Last Chance Gulch became the state capital, Helena. Virginia City was rebuilt as a typical town of the old wild West. A monument marks the lonely spot where Custer died.

In our fourth largest state, mountains cover one third of the land. Cradled in the northern ridges of the Rocky Mountains lies Glacier National Park. Its 200 lakes are as blue as the sapphires dug from Montana's hillsides. Montana is the only state where sapphires are mined.

The city of Butte is the world's largest "mining camp." Beneath Butte lies another city of mine tunnels and shafts. Here miners dig out millions of dollars' worth of copper, zinc, manganese, coal, gold, silver, and lead.

Eighty million years ago, prehistoric monsters roamed through Montana. So many dinosaur bones have been found near the town of Ekalaka that ranchers use them for doorstops! No wonder Ekalaka is called Skeleton Flats, or Fossil-town, U.S.A.

NEBRASKA

"The Cornhusker State" became the 37th State, 1867

YOU can still see rutted wheel tracks along Nebraska's Platte and Little Blue rivers. They were made by the wagons of the pioneers who followed the Platte River Valley westward on their way to Oregon and California in the 1800's. Some of them stopped when they came to Nebraska. They looked around at the grassy plains stretching, it seemed, to the sky. And they liked what they saw — good land to grow their crops. Only trees were missing. So the pioneers planted saplings around their cabins. Today two million acres of Nebraska land are covered with trees.

Most of Nebraska is farm land, and the farmers grow bumper crops of wheat, corn, and rye. In the west are Nebraska's vast ranches. Only Texas and Iowa raise more beef cattle.

There are only two large cities in Nebraska: the capital, Lincoln, named for President Lincoln, and Omaha, the major railroad center. The meat-packing industry of Omaha is one of the most important in the world. Omaha was only a camping ground in the wilderness when, in 1804, the two great explorers of the Northwest, Lewis and Clark, camped there with their Indian guides.

Long, long before Lewis and Clark paddled their boats down the Missouri River, Nebraska was explored by quite another kind of "pioneer." These were woolly mammoths, 14-foot-tall ancient ancestors of elephants. You can see their fossil remains in the University of Nebraska State Museum in Lincoln.

60

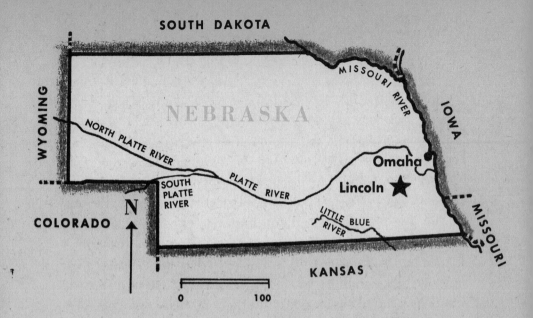

• Early Nebraska pioneers found their home a treeless prairie. They sent back East for young trees to plant. In 1872 pioneer J. S. Morton set aside Arbor Day as a special day for planting trees in Nebraska. Now Arbor Day is celebrated every year in all the states.

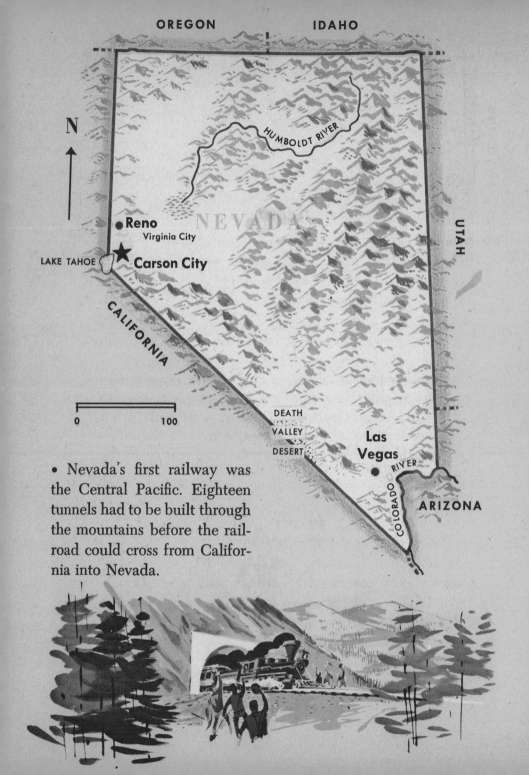

OREGON   IDAHO

N

HUMBOLDT RIVER

NEVADA

● **Reno**
Virginia City

LAKE TAHOE   ★ **Carson City**

CALIFORNIA

UTAH

0   100

DEATH
VALLEY
DESERT

**Las
Vegas** ●

COLORADO RIVER

ARIZONA

● Nevada's first railway was
the Central Pacific. Eighteen
tunnels had to be built through
the mountains before the railroad could cross from California into Nevada.

NEVADA

"The Silver State" became the 36th State, 1864

NEVADA was the last of our western states to be explored. The land seemed nothing but desert wilderness, discouraging to the homesteader. Only sagebrush grew in the valleys, and for the cattle there was only bunch grass to feed on. A small band of Mormons settled there in 1849.

Then in 1859, settlers began pouring into the lonely Nevada Territory. What drew them? The discovery of the Great Comstock Lode! The mining town of Virginia City boomed. During the next 30 years, the amazing Comstock Lode produced gold and silver worth hundreds of millions of dollars.

Nevada is one of our largest states but one of the most thinly populated. Carson City is one of the smallest state capitals. About four fifths of the population live in and around Reno and Las Vegas.

Nevada might well say of itself "How dry I am!" Less rain falls here than in any other state. The moisture-laden winds from the Pacific Ocean cannot cross its western wall of mountains—into the Great Basin. On the land, too dry to be farmed, great herds of cattle, horses, and sheep graze.

The landscape is strange and beautiful. Nevada shares with California the eerie desert of Death Valley, and deep, deep Lake Tahoe, set high in the hills. To the north are sleeping volcanoes, hot springs, and geysers. One hot spring runs into a cool mountain stream. Fishermen claim they can catch a fish in the cool stream and cook it in the hot spring without taking it off the hook!

NEW HAMPSHIRE

"The Granite State" became the 9th State, 1788

 IN 1776 New Hampshire became the first colony to set itself up as an independent state. Folks in nearby Maine and Massachusetts shook their heads in admiration, and said New Hampshirites were as tough as the granite in their White Mountains.

They *were* tough and they had good sense. They looked around and saw that their rock-ribbed, hilly state would be hard to farm. But they also saw the water power that could be harnessed from their great rivers foaming down the mountains. So the people of New Hampshire built mills and factories along the rivers. They used the rivers to turn wheels and move machinery. New Hampshire factories have been busy ever since making cloth, paper, shoes, and machine parts. And today manufacturing is the most important industry in the state.

Not everyone in New Hampshire works in factories. New Hampshire does have farms — farms that raise dairy herds, chickens and eggs. And farms that grow berries, apples, and peaches. The farmers sell many of their chickens and dairy products to New Hampshire hotels to feed hungry vacationers.

If you've ever had a New Hampshire vacation, you know why so many people go there for summer fun and winter sports. Who wouldn't enjoy hiking over green woodland trails, camping in the deep woods, or skiing down the snowy slopes of the White Mountains?

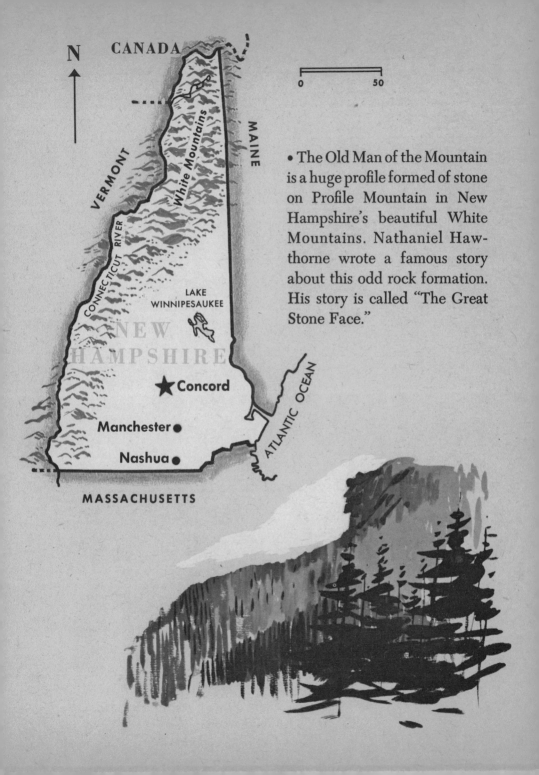

N

CANADA

VERMONT

MAINE

White Mountains

CONNECTICUT RIVER

NEW HAMPSHIRE

LAKE WINNIPESAUKEE

★ Concord

ATLANTIC OCEAN

Manchester ●

Nashua ●

MASSACHUSETTS

0   50

• The Old Man of the Mountain is a huge profile formed of stone on Profile Mountain in New Hampshire's beautiful White Mountains. Nathaniel Hawthorne wrote a famous story about this odd rock formation. His story is called "The Great Stone Face."

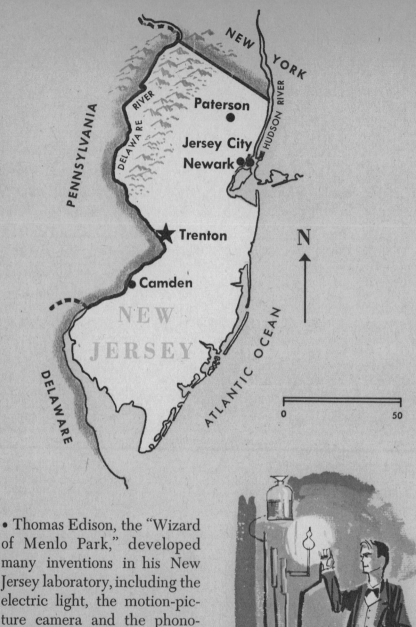

N

0   50

• Thomas Edison, the "Wizard of Menlo Park," developed many inventions in his New Jersey laboratory, including the electric light, the motion-picture camera and the phonograph. Edison's laboratory and machine shop are open to interested visitors.

NEW JERSEY

"The Garden State" became the 3rd State, 1787

FARMS and factories, superhighways and dirt roads, mountains and beaches, port cities and fishing villages — you can find them all in New Jersey, one of our smallest states.

New Jersey — between the Delaware River and the sea — is almost an island. Ocean-going ships come upriver as far as Camden and Trenton. Freighters, ocean liners, and tankers dock in the broad harbors of Newark, Jersey City, and Hoboken, which are part of the busiest port in the world — the port of New York.

New Jersey has at least 50 million neighbors, including the people of New York City and Philadelphia. These good neighbors are good customers, too. They buy the products of New Jersey's factories and farms.

These products are astonishingly varied. The oil in your furnace, the paint and varnish on your furniture, your mother's electric iron, and canned soup — your radio, too — may have come from New Jersey. No other state produces so many chemical products. Manufacturing is by far New Jersey's most important business, but the "Garden State" raises all kinds of crops, too. It is said that New Jersey farms produce everything from A to Z — from apples to zucchini!

During the Revolutionary War, George Washington's army won its first victory at Trenton in New Jersey. On Christmas night in 1776, Washington ferried his troops across the icy Delaware River and gave the enemy soldiers an unexpected Christmas surprise.

NEW MEXICO

"Land of Enchantment" became the 47th State, 1912

SQUARE-SHAPED New Mexico is a combination of the old and the new, of Indian, Spanish, and American ways of life. Navajo and Pueblo Indians were here long before the Spaniard Coronado came in 1540. Today one hears both English and Spanish in New Mexico.

In New Mexico one is always reminded of the past. In Gallup, Indians still dance their ancient tribal dances. In Santa Fe, oldest capital city in the U.S., there are buildings 350 years old. Signs of the future are just as strong. In the desert at White Sands, scientists experiment with rockets. At the Lovelace Clinic in Albuquerque, they test the astronauts, our first space men.

You don't often need a raincoat in sunny New Mexico. This is a dry land and water is very precious. The Rio Grande flows across the state, and its waters help irrigate the farms that grow corn, wheat, and cotton.

Sheep and cattle raising are important here. So is mining for copper, lead, silver, and gold. New Mexico leads the nation in the production of uranium, the raw material for atomic energy. It produces the most potash, too.

Almost anywhere in New Mexico you can see her mountain peaks. Children who go to the public schools in Santa Fe get skiing lessons in the Sangre de Cristo Mountains.

In this "Land of Enchantment" one of the most magical places is Carlsbad Caverns. This is the largest group of connected underground caves ever discovered. Scientists say they were formed 60 million years ago.

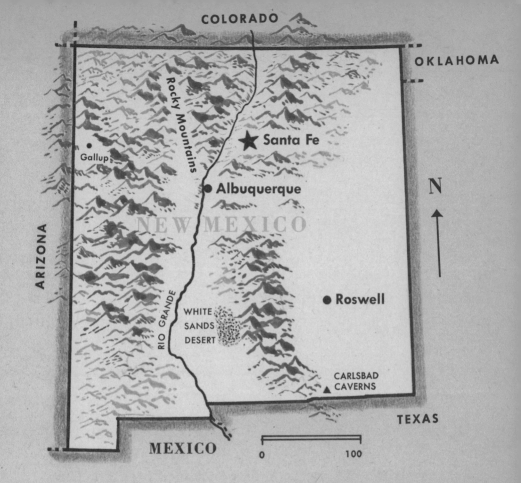

COLORADO

OKLAHOMA

Rocky Mountains

★ Santa Fe

Gallup

● Albuquerque

NEW MEXICO

N

ARIZONA

RIO GRANDE

WHITE
SANDS
DESERT

● Roswell

CARLSBAD
CAVERNS ▲

TEXAS

MEXICO

0   100

• Long before Columbus found the New World, Indians built pueblo villages in New Mexico. Made of sun-dried brick, these pueblos rose like "apartment houses" on flat-topped hills. To get from one level to another, ladders were used. Some pueblos had as many as a thousand rooms. Zuni and Hopi Indians today live in pueblos as their ancestors did.

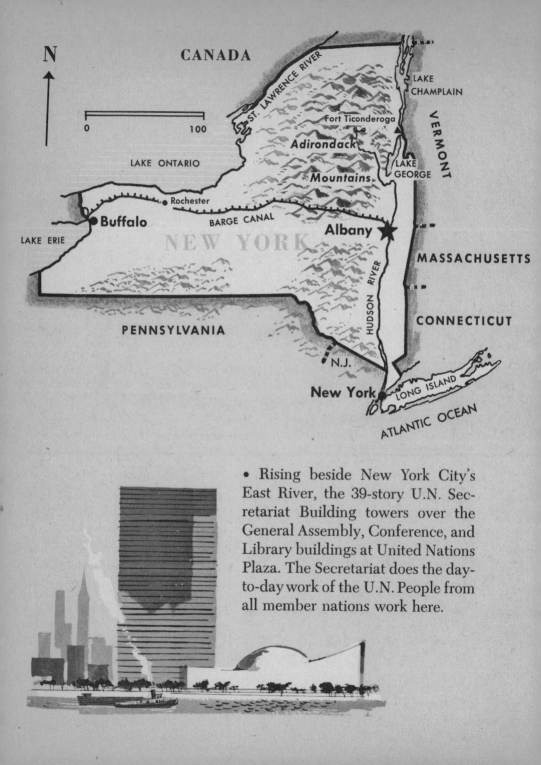

N

CANADA

ST. LAWRENCE RIVER

LAKE CHAMPLAIN

0   100

LAKE ONTARIO

Fort Ticonderoga

Adirondack

VERMONT

LAKE GEORGE

Mountains

Rochester

Buffalo

BARGE CANAL

Albany ★

NEW YORK

LAKE ERIE

MASSACHUSETTS

CONNECTICUT

HUDSON RIVER

PENNSYLVANIA

N.J.

New York

LONG ISLAND

ATLANTIC OCEAN

• Rising beside New York City's East River, the 39-story U.N. Secretariat Building towers over the General Assembly, Conference, and Library buildings at United Nations Plaza. The Secretariat does the day-to-day work of the U.N. People from all member nations work here.

NEW YORK

"The Empire State" became the 11th State, 1788

 IN 1626 the Dutch bought Manhattan Island from the Indians. Guess what they paid? Twenty-four dollars. Guess what that land is worth today? Thirty billion dollars! For Manhattan is now the business center of New York City — the largest city in the Americas.

New York's harbor handles more freight than any other port in the Western Hemisphere, and there are always at least 150 ships at her piers. New York City has the most hotels, museums, broadcasting stations, clothing factories, banks, and publishing houses of any city in America. Here, too, are the Empire State Building — one of the world's tallest buildings — the Statue of Liberty, and the United Nations.

More than a third of the battles of the Revolutionary War were fought in New York State. After the war, many settlers moved to the fertile inland valleys of central and western New York. Later they shipped their produce to eastern cities along the Erie Canal on barges towed by horses. Expanded and deepened, the Erie is now part of New York's great Barge Canal. Tugs do the work that horses used to do.

New York State has more than a dozen major industrial cities. But vineyards and orchards flourish in its valleys, and its dairy farms rank high in milk production. New York City attracts the most visitors, but vacationers also throng to the state's lovely lakes and mountains.

For 150 years the Empire State had the largest population of any state, but in 1963 California took first place. How many people live in New York State? More than 18 million! Most nations of the world do not have so large a population.

NORTH CAROLINA

"The Tar Heel State" became the 12th State, 1789

THE first English colony in North America was a lost colony. Even before the Jamestown settlement, even before the Pilgrims landed on Plymouth Rock, English ships had sailed to the coast of what is now North Carolina. They brought a colony of 150 people who settled on Roanoke Island. When the ships returned three years later, everyone in the colony had vanished — including Virginia Dare, the first child born of English parents in America.

Many a ship was lost, too, off the dangerous North Carolina coast. Sailors had good reason to fear stormy Cape Hatteras, which they called the "Graveyard of the Atlantic."

The coast of North Carolina may be stormy, but inland the landscape is peaceful and lovely. In the east are fertile plains, and rising in the west are the Appalachian Mountains. With neighboring Tennessee, North Carolina shares one of the most popular vacation sites in the nation — Great Smoky Mountains National Park. The smoky blue haze over the mountains gives the Smokies their name.

Only Texas has more farms than North Carolina. And on this rich land, farmers raise cotton, corn, tobacco, soybeans, fruit, and peanuts. North Carolina scientists have developed an atomic peanut. They call it NC 4X. These extra-large peanuts are grown from seeds exposed to atomic radiation.

No other state produces so much tobacco, textiles, and softwood lumber. So it's not surprising that North Carolina also has the largest hosiery mills and cigarette factories in the world, and makes much of the nation's furniture.

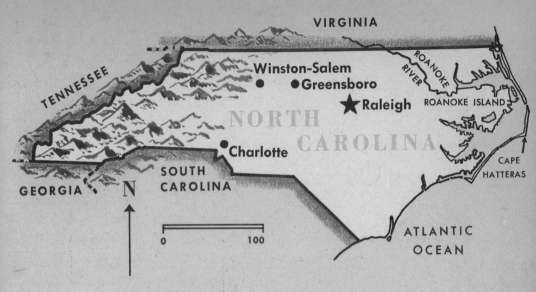

VIRGINIA

TENNESSEE

Winston-Salem
●Greensboro
●Raleigh ★

NORTH

Charlotte●

CAROLINA

SOUTH
CAROLINA

GEORGIA

ROANOKE RIVER

ROANOKE ISLAND

CAPE
HATTERAS

ATLANTIC
OCEAN

N

0   100

• The first flight in a power-driven airplane was made by Wilbur and Orville Wright on December 17, 1903. It took place at Kitty Hawk Beach near Roanoke Island. This flight lasted only 12 seconds. Five years later Wilbur set a new world's record by flying a plane 52 miles and staying aloft for over an hour. A monument stands at Kill Devil Hill near Kitty Hawk Beach to mark the scene of the first plane flight.

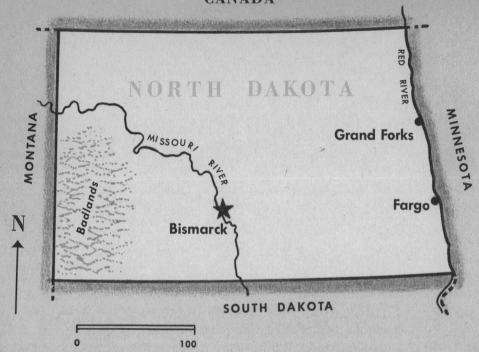

NORTH DAKOTA

MONTANA

RED RIVER

MINNESOTA

MISSOURI RIVER

Grand Forks

Badlands

Bismarck

Fargo

N

SOUTH DAKOTA

0   100

• Sacagawea was a young Indian squaw. In 1804, she joined the expedition of Lewis and Clark not far from where Bismarck stands today. She guided them, helped them deal with the Indians, and led them safely across the mountains. This statue of Sacagawea stands on the Capitol grounds at Bismarck.

NORTH DAKOTA

"Flickertail State" became the 39th or 40th State, 1889

THE Great Dakota Mystery will never be solved. Until 1889 North and South Dakota made up the Dakota Territory. Then both joined the Union at the same time as separate states. Which one was admitted first? No one will ever know. For President Harrison deliberately shuffled the two state proclamations before signing them.

Before 1850 farming was difficult in much of North Dakota. Then it was discovered that wheat would flourish in the Red River Valley. Soon railroads were built to bring in the thousands of settlers who came to farm the vast prairies. Ever since, the Red River Valley has been one of the great wheat-growing regions of the world.

The ranches of North Dakota are big, too. Although there is snow in the winter, cattle and sheep can range all year. The sweet clover blossoms that grow on the plains have made possible a profitable bee-keeping industry.

The broad Missouri River can be seen from the 18-story Capitol building in Bismarck. There is still a log cabin on these modern Capitol grounds — the cabin where Theodore Roosevelt lived during 1883.

So weird are some of the stone peaks in the Badlands of North Dakota that the Dakota Indians believed there were demons lurking among them. Near Amidon, beds of lignite (a sort of half-made coal) burn like an underground furnace, giving off a reddish glow at night that can be seen for miles around.

OHIO

"The Buckeye State" became the 17th State, 1803

FOR almost two hundred years, Ohio was the crossroads of a growing America. Pioneers came by canoe across Lake Erie, by barge and keelboat down the Ohio River. They came from the South and they came from New England. The New Englanders called their new Ohio towns by the names they had left behind — Norwalk and New London. The southerners built white-pillared homes in towns they called Gambier and Mount Vernon. And beside Lake Erie, Moses Cleaveland built a town.

Cleveland is now Ohio's largest city and the state's chief steel-making center. Although Ohio has no iron of its own, steel is a major industry. The iron ore brought by way of Lake Erie feeds the great steel mills of Cleveland, Steubenville, Youngstown, Lorain, and Canton.

Ohio and industry go hand in hand. Columbus, the capital city, produces aircraft and machinery. Cincinnati, busy port on the Ohio River, has a large printing industry. Dayton makes the nation's cash registers, and Toledo its scales. From Akron come most of the tires for America's cars.

Ohio is rich in natural resources — coal, limestone, oil, and timber. Toledo is one of the most important coal-shipping ports in the world. And from the clay deposits come the pottery and porcelain for which Ohio's southeastern cities are famous. The soil, too, is rich and yields a harvest of corn, fruit, dairy products, and tobacco.

Ohio has sent eight of its sons to the White House — Grant, Hayes, Garfield, McKinley, Taft, Harding, and two Harrisons.

MICHIGAN

LAKE ERIE

PENNSYLVANIA

Toledo

Lorain Cleveland

Akron ●
Youngstown

OHIO

INDIANA

Steubenville ●

★ Columbus

Dayton
●

Cincinnati

WEST VIRGINIA

OHIO RIVER

KENTUCKY

N

0   100

• Ohio has been a fruit-growing state since
pioneer days when "Johnny Appleseed" wan-
dered through the territory, planting his apple
trees. His real name was John Chapman.

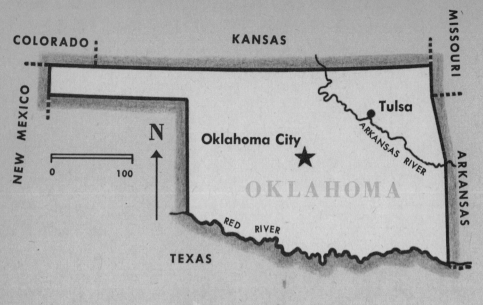

COLORADO · KANSAS · MISSOURI

NEW MEXICO

N

0   100

Oklahoma City ★

Tulsa ●

ARKANSAS RIVER

ARKANSAS

OKLAHOMA

RED RIVER

TEXAS

• You could almost spell Oklahoma O-I-L! There's so much oil that oil-well derricks even dot the Capitol grounds in Oklahoma City. One big oil strike took place in 1920 on land held by the Osage Indians.

OKLAHOMA

"The Sooner State" became the 46th State, 1907

IT IS April 22, 1889. In wagons and prairie schooners, eager homesteaders wait for a pistol shot. Crack! The Oklahoma Territory is open! The rush for land is on. Within twenty-four hours 50,000 settlers have staked their claims. Some homesteaders jumped the gun, however, and entered the territory sooner. That is how Oklahoma earned its nickname — the Sooner State.

It was the Indians, though, who named Oklahoma. The name came from their word for *Land of the Red People.* When parts of the territory were opened to white settlers, the Indians were moved to land in Oklahoma that no one wanted. It was a lucky move. In 1920 oil was discovered on this very land.

Oil is now Oklahoma's most important business. More than 700 petroleum companies have their headquarters in Tulsa, often called "The Oil Capital of the World." And in Oklahoma City, the capital, people have even discovered oil in their back yards!

Oklahoma is rich in other minerals, too — natural gas, coal, and zinc. And her fertile farms yield wheat, rye, cotton, and the largest crop of broomcorn in the U. S. On the ranches of Oklahoma, cowboys herd cattle, sheep, horses — even turkeys! Cowboys are so important in Oklahoma that a monument dedicated to them stands in front of the Capitol building in Oklahoma City.

Oklahoma is shaped somewhat like a saucepan. Doesn't the narrow strip to the west look like the handle of the pan? That's what it's called — the *Panhandle.*

OREGON

"The Beaver State" became the 33rd State, 1859

NOT long ago a skeleton was dug up in central Oregon. It was the skeleton of a mighty brontosaurus — fifty feet from head to tail! Perhaps it lived on the giant palms and ferns that flourished when Oregon was a prehistoric jungle.

In those ancient times the highest mountains were volcanoes, and a terrific volcanic explosion blew the top off one great mountain peak. The hole which it left, almost half a mile deep, is filled today with the blue waters of Crater Lake. Oregon's highest peak is an inactive volcano called Mt. Hood. It is not far from Oregon's most active and largest city, Portland.

From the dense forests that cover the lower slopes of Oregon's mountains come much of America's lumber. Under parts of these forests lie treasures of gold and silver.

Oregon's Snake River has the deepest canyon in the country. Irrigation projects in the Snake River Valley have turned a desert into fertile grain- and vegetable-growing country. Western Oregon is one of the world's great fruit-growing regions.

The great Columbia River, which the Indians called *Ouragan,* serves Oregon well. The huge Bonneville Dam on the Columbia generates electric power for homes and factories.

The Dam has also helped make the Columbia an important river highway, for ocean-going ships can now sail inland 100 miles, past Portland. The Columbia River is also a "highway" for the many thousands of salmon that keep Oregon's fisheries and canneries busy. Fish ladders — a step-like series of pools — help the salmon go upstream past the Columbia's dams.

• In the 1840's and '50's, thousands of pioneers took the Oregon Trail, bound for free land in Oregon's Willamette Valley. The trail — 2,000 hard, dangerous miles — was America's longest overland route. Parts of it, rutted by wagon wheels, can still be seen.

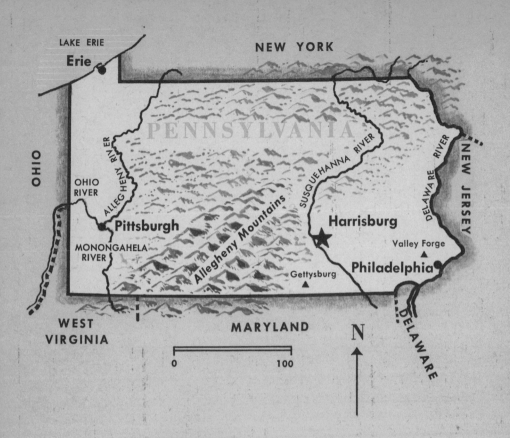

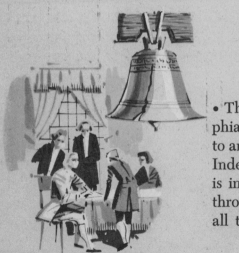

• The Liberty Bell in Philadelphia's Independence Hall rang to announce the Declaration of Independence in 1776. The bell is inscribed: "Proclaim liberty throughout all the land, unto all the inhabitants thereof."

PENNSYLVANIA

"The Keystone State" became the 2nd State, 1787

The riddle: Why is Philadelphia's City Hall called the biggest penholder in the world?

The answer: Because the top of the City Hall holds a statue of William Penn that's 37 feet tall!

William Penn is tall indeed in the history of this state. A Quaker himself, he founded a colony where all could worship as they pleased. That's why he chose the name Philadelphia, which means "brotherly love," for his first settlement. Philadelphia is now our fourth largest city.

Meet another citizen of Pennsylvania — Mike Fink the keelboatman, born in Pittsburgh about 1770. Many a pioneer heading west or south was carried down the Ohio River on Mike's keelboat. Today the Ohio carries freight barges laden with iron and steel from Pittsburgh's great mills.

Pennsylvania is one of the top-ranking industrial states in the Union. About one fourth of the nation's steel is produced here, and only West Virginia and Kentucky mine more coal. Pennsylvania's hills are rich in other minerals, too — in oil and natural gas, iron and limestone.

And American history has roots deep in Pennsylvania soil. At Valley Forge, George Washington held together a cold and hungry army in the cruelest winter of the Revolutionary War. The Declaration of Independence was adopted in Philadelphia's Independence Hall. And it was in dedicating the bloody battleground of Gettysburg that Abraham Lincoln told the world that "government of the people, by the people, for the people, shall not perish from the earth."

RHODE ISLAND

"*Little Rhody*" became the 13th State, 1790

HOW SMALL is our smallest state? Only 48 miles long and 37 miles wide! You could fit 220 Rhode Islands into Texas! But if you compared one average square mile in each of our states, you'd find that Rhode Island is the second most densely populated state in the Union.

Rhode Island has a proud history, and was founded on a great freedom — the freedom of worship. In 1636 Roger Williams established the settlement of Providence and offered shelter to all who wished to worship in their own way. In the struggle for independence, Rhode Islanders played a bold role. In 1772, when the British ship *Gaspee* came to collect taxes, they set the ship afire. So impatient were Rhode Islanders to be free, they announced their independence of British rule three months before the Declaration of Independence was accepted by the Continental Congress. Later they passed the first law in America forbidding the bringing in of slaves from Africa. There is a statue atop the Capitol building in Providence called Independent Man. He seems the very spirit of Rhode Island!

The state is small and its farmland poor, and most Rhode Islanders turned to business and manufacturing to make a living. Manufacturing history was made when the first cotton-spinning mill in America went into operation at Pawtucket in 1790. Today the making of textiles is Rhode Island's leading industry. Other factories turn out machinery and rubber goods, and "Little Rhody" is one of the leading states in the making of silverware and jewelry.

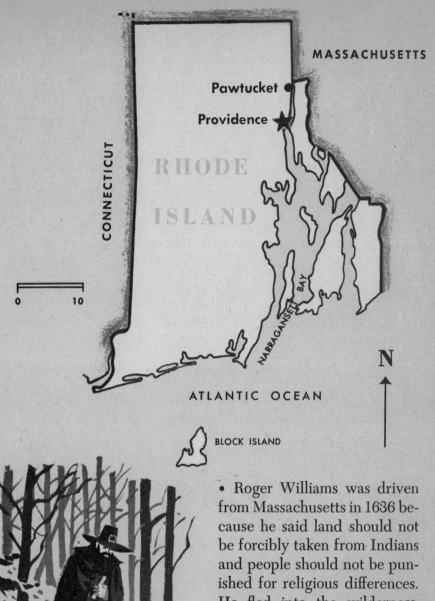

MASSACHUSETTS

Pawtucket

Providence

CONNECTICUT

RHODE

ISLAND

0   10

Narragansett Bay

ATLANTIC OCEAN

N

BLOCK ISLAND

• Roger Williams was driven from Massachusetts in 1636 because he said land should not be forcibly taken from Indians and people should not be punished for religious differences. He fled into the wilderness, where friendly Indians gave him land on which he founded Rhode Island. Williams' colony was the first to grant complete freedom of worship to all.

• South Carolina became the first state to secede from the Union when Lincoln was elected in 1860. The first shot of the Civil War was fired on Fort Sumter in Charleston Harbor on April 12, 1861.

SOUTH CAROLINA

"The Palmetto State" became the 8th State, 1788

 PIRATE ground! In the 1700's South Carolina's inlets and marshes and islands were hideouts for Blackbeard and other bloodthirsty buccaneers.

In those days English settlers brought roots and seeds to plant in the fertile soil of the new colony. On the plantations that sprawled beyond the lovely town of Charleston, colonists raised rice and the indigo used to make blue dyes.

Today Charleston is a beautiful port city with many formal gardens and mansions, some more than 200 years old. Ships sail out of her busy harbors crammed with bales of cotton, for cotton has long been one of South Carolina's leading crops. Much of this cotton stays behind in South Carolina, however, to be made into cloth. Huge cotton crops and cheap water power from swift-running rivers have helped to make South Carolina one of the nation's leading textile manufacturers. Her busy mills produce wool, rayon, nylon, and orlon, as well as cotton fabrics.

Rich soil makes it possible for South Carolina farmers to harvest tobacco, soybeans, peaches, oats, peanuts, and corn. They raise hogs, cows, and chickens, too. And at Sumter there is a pigeon farm which is said to be the largest in the world.

The British colony of Carolina was named for Charles I. So was Charleston. But the "Palmetto State" won its nickname *fighting* a British king — George III. In a fort built of palmetto logs on an island in South Carolina a small band of patriots won the first victory of the Revolutionary War.

SOUTH DAKOTA

"Coyote State" became the 39th or 40th State, 1889*

 SOUTH DAKOTA's bones are world famous! For strange creatures once lived there — tiny three-toed horses and saber-toothed tigers. Their fossilized bones have been found in the White River Badlands, and shown in museums around the world. The Badlands are famous, too — over a million acres of weird landscape.

The Missouri River flows through South Dakota for more than 500 miles, almost cutting the state in two. To the west of the river are the plains and great ranches where wheat is grown and herds of cattle and sheep graze. East of the Missouri, the soil is fertile and the rainfall good. Flat fields of wheat, corn, rye, and oats seem to stretch to the sky's edge. Flax, soybeans, and apples grow well here, too.

In the southwest are the beautiful Black Hills. They might well have been called "Gold Hills." Custer's men discovered gold here in 1874, and since then these mountains have yielded precious metal worth millions of dollars. Homestake Mine, at Lead, is one of the largest gold mines in the world.

Today visitors come to the Black Hills to see the largest sculptures ever made by man. These are the huge stone faces of Washington, Jefferson, Lincoln, and Theodore Roosevelt. Carved out of the granite sides of Mount Rushmore, the carved faces are in proportion to men 465 feet tall.

South Dakota's capital, Pierre, was once a small trading post, and the first governor of South Dakota was William Jayne. Governor Jayne was also a doctor. Who was his most famous patient? Abraham Lincoln!

*See North Dakota, p. 75.

• *Calamity Jane,* whose real name was Martha Jane Canary, got her nickname because she claimed that to offend her was to "court calamity." She was an expert at riding, shooting, and fighting. She could drive a mule team like the best of the "mule skinners." Her good friend in Deadwood was Wild Bill Hickok.

MISSOURI · ARKANSAS · MISSISSIPPI RIVER · KENTUCKY · VIRGINIA · NORTH CAROLINA · Nashville · Knoxville · TENNESSEE · TENNESSEE RIVER · Memphis · Chattanooga · MISSISSIPPI · ALABAMA · GEORGIA · N · 0 100

• Davy Crockett was born in the Great Smoky Mountains in east Tennessee, in 1786. He served his country as a soldier and Indian scout. Tennessee voters elected him to Congress three times. His motto, "Be sure you're right, then go ahead," became known all over the nation.

TENNESSEE

"The Volunteer State" became the 16th State, 1796

THE three stars in Tennessee's flag stand for three parts of the state. If you ask a native of Tennessee where he lives he may say East or Middle or West Tennessee. In the *East* rise the Great Smoky Mountains. Here mountaineers farm their crops on hills so steep that harvests often have to be hauled away on sleds. Coal deposits are found in East Tennessee, too. *Middle Tennessee,* lying in the Cumberland foothills, is rolling and hilly. Here cattle, sheep and horses graze on grassy land. *Western Tennessee,* between the Mississippi and the winding, bending Tennessee River, is a land of white cotton fields.

The rich valleys of Tennessee always drew the farmers, even in pioneer days. In time the soil became less fertile. Too much cotton raising wore out the land. Floods washed away the rich topsoil. In 1933 Congress set up TVA — the Tennessee Valley Authority. TVA built dams to control the floods and restore the land. TVA also created water power for new industries. Today factories along the river banks process food, make chemicals, and manufacture textiles. Tennessee also produces marble and other important minerals, including coal and zinc.

Tennessee has four cities where more than 100,000 people live — Memphis, Nashville, Chattanooga, and Knoxville. The newest city in the state is Oak Ridge, near Knoxville. Here, in the greatest secrecy, part of the first atomic bomb was made. The project was so secret people didn't even know there *was* an Oak Ridge until the end of World War II.

TEXAS

"The Lone Star State" became the 28th State, 1845

 TEXAS was once an independent nation. It became a republic after General Sam Houston defeated the Mexican forces in 1836. Shortly after, Texas elected Sam Houston president of the "Republic of Texas" and named its largest city, Houston, in his honor.

You need the word LARGE to describe Texas. Texas is our second largest state. The largest state fair is held in Dallas every October and in the nearby city of Tyler is the largest rose-growing center in the world. The largest state capitol building is at Austin, capital of Texas. And the irrigation program in Texas is vast, too — with many large projects along the coast and in the lower Rio Grande below Falcon Dam.

You need the word MOST, too. For Texas has the most farms in the U. S. and raises the most cattle and sheep on its great ranches. Texas grows the most cotton and vegetables, and produces a third of the nation's oil.

Remember the Alamo? The famous old mission building known as "The Alamo" still stands in San Antonio. Here Davy Crockett, Jim Bowie, and other brave men fought to the death for the freedom of Texas.

There were pirates as well as heroes in Texas' past. The buccaneer Jean Lafitte founded a town that became the port city of Galveston on the Gulf of Mexico. Galveston Island was his headquarters until the U. S. Navy drove him out.

There's only one star in the flag of the Lone Star State. But it stands for stirring moments in American history.

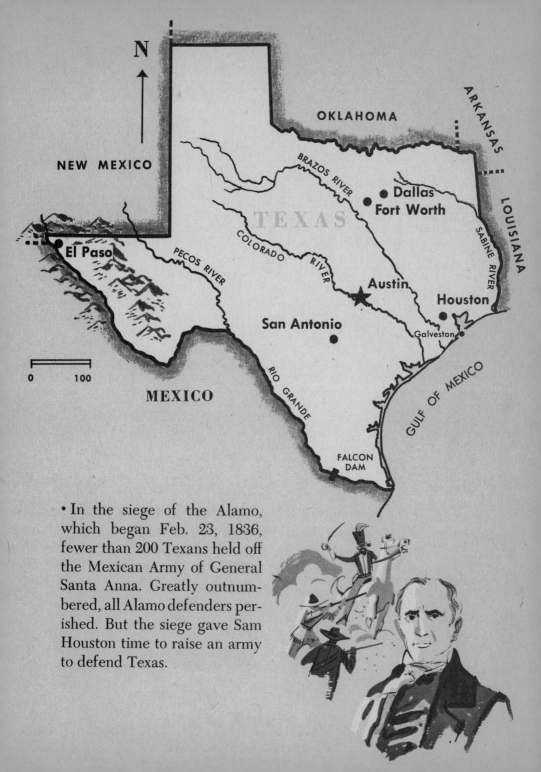

N

NEW MEXICO

OKLAHOMA

ARKANSAS

LOUISIANA

TEXAS

BRAZOS RIVER

● Dallas
Fort Worth

El Paso

PECOS RIVER

COLORADO RIVER

SABINE RIVER

Austin

Houston ●

San Antonio ●

Galveston

0   100

MEXICO

RIO GRANDE

GULF OF MEXICO

FALCON
DAM

• In the siege of the Alamo, which began Feb. 23, 1836, fewer than 200 Texans held off the Mexican Army of General Santa Anna. Greatly outnumbered, all Alamo defenders perished. But the siege gave Sam Houston time to raise an army to defend Texas.

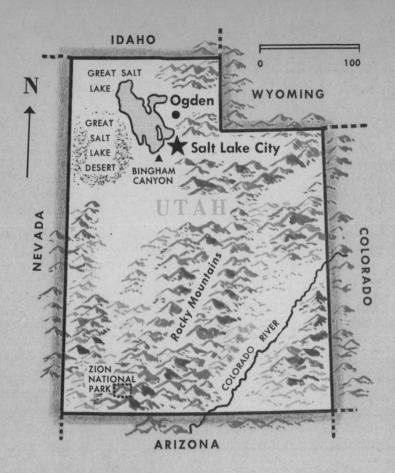

IDAHO

N

GREAT SALT
LAKE

Ogden

GREAT
SALT
LAKE
DESERT

BINGHAM
CANYON

★ Salt Lake City

WYOMING

0   100

NEVADA

UTAH

Rocky Mountains

COLORADO RIVER

COLORADO

ZION
NATIONAL
PARK

ARIZONA

• James Bridger, fur trapper and scout, was the first white man to see Utah's Great Salt Lake. When he came upon the lake's vast stretches of shining water in 1824, Bridger thought at first that he had reached the shores of the Pacific.

UTAH

"The Beehive State" became the 45th State, 1896

THE Great Salt Lake valley stretching ahead seemed nothing but desert and mountains. But to the band of weary Mormons, seeking freedom of worship, it was the promised land. "This is the place," said Brigham Young, their leader. The Mormons unhitched their oxen and started planting potatoes. They dammed up a stream and dug ditches and channels so water would flow to where it was needed. That was in 1847.

The Mormons made the Utah desert blossom with their irrigation methods. Today thousands of acres of fertile soil produce grains, fruits, and vegetables. But manufacturing is Utah's most important industry, with food and metal products leading the parade. Gold, silver, lead, zinc, uranium, coal — her hills are filled with treasure. Especially copper! There's a mountain of copper ore at Bingham Canyon.

Utah is an inland state, far from the Atlantic and Pacific oceans. Then where does that good sea smell of salty air come from? From the clear, green waters of Great Salt Lake near Salt Lake City—waters saltier than the ocean. Swimming there is fun, for you can't sink. The salt keeps you afloat.

Utah has many other natural wonders, carved and shaped by wind and water. Rainbow Bridge in southeastern Utah is the largest natural bridge in the world. And strangely colored canyons, deserts, and gorges fill the National Parks — Zion Park and Bryce Canyon — with weird beauty.

Utah's weather is a natural wonder, too — clear and dry 300 days out of the year.

VERMONT

"Green Mountain State" became the 14th State, 1791

 VERMONT is well-named. It was the French, led by Champlain, who first explored here, and in their language *vert mont* means *green mountain.*

Fast-running streams and rivers tumble down these green mountains — rivers that mean water power for Vermont's factories. From these factories come machine tools, weighing scales, and textiles. From Vermont's forests and sawmills and wood-working plants come lumber and pulp for the making of paper. And in her hills are layers of asbestos, slate and fine building stone. United Nations headquarters in New York City was built of Vermont marble, and the state's own handsome Capitol at Montpelier is made of native granite.

Despite its rocky soil, Vermont does much farming. Vermont's maple syrup is famous everywhere. Indians made the first syrup. They notched the maple trees and caught the sweet sap in birchbark buckets. Today many Vermont farmers have sugar maple trees. The Indians would be astonished by the plastic pipes and tin containers used today, but they would recognize the old delicious flavor. You can see Vermont "sugaring" from early March to mid-April.

Vermont is a favorite vacation place. People come to see the peaceful farms and historic towns. They camp in the mountains in the summer and ski down its trails in the winter.

Some visitors return to stay. Rudyard Kipling liked Vermont so much he built a home in Brattleboro where he wrote for many years. Have you ever read *The Jungle Book?* The story took place in India but Kipling wrote it in Vermont!

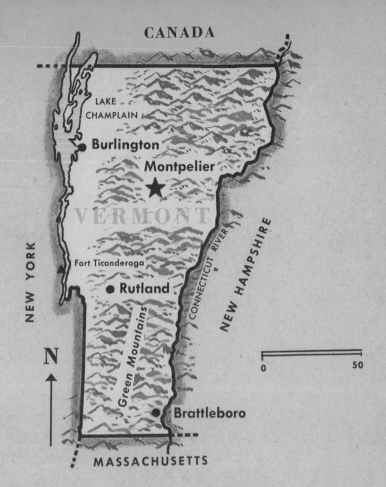

CANADA

LAKE CHAMPLAIN

Burlington

Montpelier ★

VERMONT

NEW YORK

Fort Ticonderoga

Rutland

CONNECTICUT RIVER

NEW HAMPSHIRE

Green Mountains

N

0   50

Brattleboro

MASSACHUSETTS

• At dawn on May 10, 1775, Ethan Allen and his Green Mountain Boys — volunteers from Vermont — captured Fort Ticonderoga, New York, from the surprised and sleepy British. Allen is said to have demanded their surrender "in the name of the Great Jehovah and the Continental Congress."

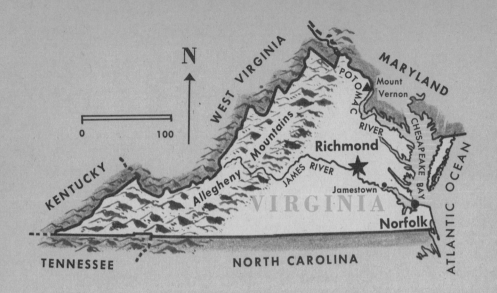

N

0   100

WEST VIRGINIA

KENTUCKY

Allegheny Mountains

JAMES RIVER

POTOMAC RIVER

MARYLAND

Mount Vernon

CHESAPEAKE BAY

Richmond

VIRGINIA

Jamestown

Norfolk

ATLANTIC OCEAN

TENNESSEE

NORTH CAROLINA

• George Washington's happiest years were spent on his estate at Mount Vernon, overlooking the Potomac River. There as a gentleman farmer he grew large crops of grain and tobacco. Visitors to Mount Vernon today can wander through the rooms of Washington's stately home, furnished as they were when he lived there.

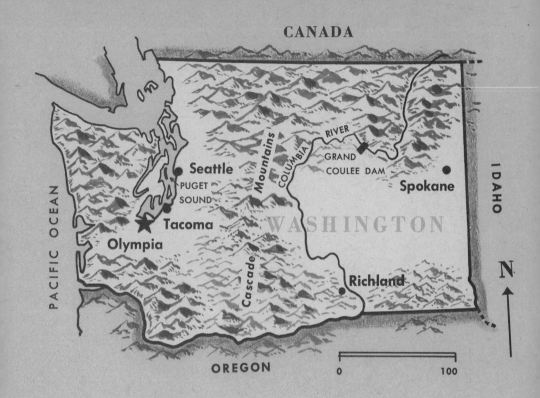

CANADA

Mountains

COLUMBIA

RIVER

GRAND
COULEE DAM

Seattle

PUGET
SOUND

Spokane

IDAHO

PACIFIC OCEAN

Tacoma

Olympia

WASHINGTON

Cascade

Richland

N

OREGON

0   100

• Washington is famous for its sockeye salmon fishing and for its other fishing industries. Seattle, one of the largest salmon markets in the world, handles fish from both Washington and Alaska.

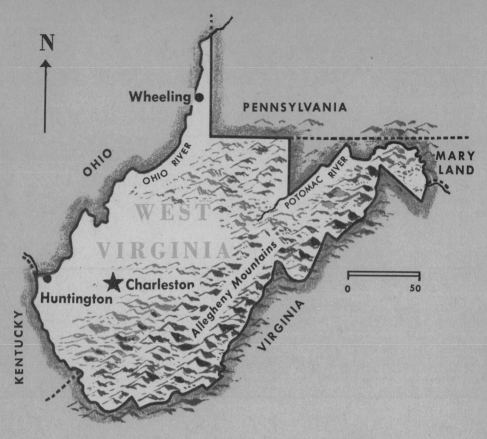

• Coal deposits lie under some two thirds of West Virginia's rocky surface. Many West Virginia workers earn their living by mining coal. Coal was first discovered in the state by John Salley in 1742 and was in use about 1810 to heat homes and make steel in Wheeling.

WEST VIRGINIA

"The Mountain State" became the 35th State, 1863

 UNTIL 1861, West Virginia was a region in Virginia, separated from the rest of the state by the Allegheny Mountains. When the Civil War began, Virginia became part of the Confederacy. West Virginia seceded from Virginia and joined the Union as a separate state.

If a reporter had interviewed the first West Virginia settlers, he might have reported this conversation:

"How do you plan to make a living here?"

"We'll start farms. Most of us are farmers."

"But there's not much level ground. Look around you — hills and mountains everywhere."

"Then we'll plant our crops on the slopes. Where we can't plant, we'll graze our cattle and hogs and sheep. Those of us who don't farm might go into the salt business. We've watched the Indians make salt from salt-water pools. We've seen them collect all the salt left after the pools dried up."

Today West Virginia's salt deposits are necessary to one of its largest industries — the manufacture of chemicals. West Virginia still farms — especially fruit. Part of the Shenandoah Valley, one of the largest apple-growing areas in America, crosses the northeastern tip of the state.

In West Virginia they tell tall tales about John Henry, the steel-driving man — John Henry, who drove the steel for the Big Bend railroad tunnel up in the Allegheny Mountains.

And there are many tunnels in the mountains of West Virginia. Most of them lead into the sunless corridors of coal mines, for West Virginia produces the most soft, or bituminous, coal in the nation.

WISCONSIN

"The Badger State" became the 30th State, 1848

 WATER, water everywhere! Three important rivers run through this state, and there are more than 8,000 lakes. And now, thanks to the St. Lawrence Seaway, Wisconsin's Great Lakes cities are linked by water to the sea.

Wisconsin is famous as the "Dairyland of the Nation," for she produces more milk and cheese than any other state. Have you ever heard of cheese-wrestling? No, it isn't a sport, and you won't see it on TV. It's part of the work of cheese-making in the city of Monroe. There workers really "wrestle" big 250-pound wheels of cheese as they rub them with salt.

Wisconsin does have plenty of sports — skiing and ice-boating in winter, fishing and hunting all year round. The state has many kinds of game birds and animals. But oddly enough its nickname comes not from badger-hunting, but from lead-mining. Years ago, lead miners in southwest Wisconsin were called "badgers." They lived in caves that reminded people of badgers' burrows.

Wisconsin's state government has been a leader in the making of laws to improve working and living conditions. It was the first state to pass laws providing pensions for mothers and teachers, payments to workers injured on their jobs, payments to unemployed people, and pensions for old people. Wisconsin has also been a leader in setting up co-operatives where people could buy and sell goods at a saving.

Fox Indians called the part of Wisconsin they lived in *"Delightful Land."* This area is now Milwaukee, Wisconsin's largest city and a leading Great Lakes port.

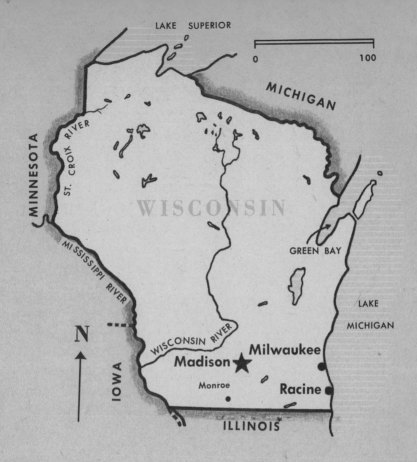

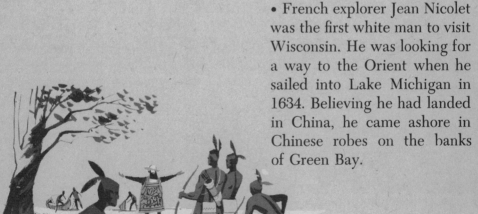

• French explorer Jean Nicolet was the first white man to visit Wisconsin. He was looking for a way to the Orient when he sailed into Lake Michigan in 1634. Believing he had landed in China, he came ashore in Chinese robes on the banks of Green Bay.

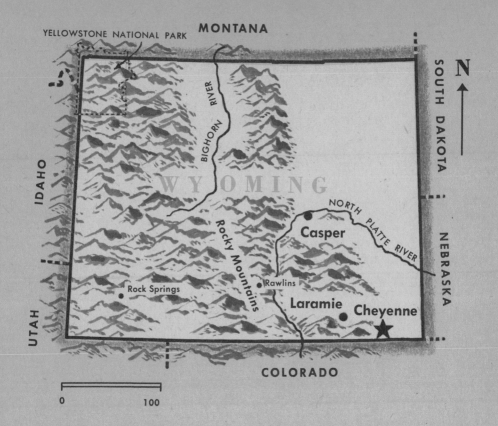

MONTANA

YELLOWSTONE NATIONAL PARK

N

IDAHO

SOUTH DAKOTA

BIGHORN RIVER

WYOMING

NEBRASKA

NORTH PLATTE RIVER

Casper

Rocky Mountains

Rock Springs

Rawlins

Laramie

Cheyenne

UTAH

COLORADO

0   100

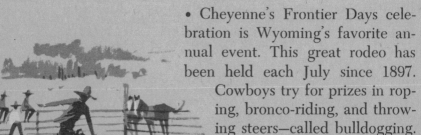

• Cheyenne's Frontier Days celebration is Wyoming's favorite annual event. This great rodeo has been held each July since 1897. Cowboys try for prizes in roping, bronco-riding, and throwing steers—called bulldogging.

WYOMING

"The Equality State" became the 44th State, 1890

JETS of hot water shoot hundreds of feet into the air. Streams of cold water and streams of boiling water run side by side down high mountains. Where is this land of fire and ice? In Yellowstone National Park in Wyoming, a region of spouting geysers, mountains, rivers, and lakes.

Less than a hundred years ago, Wyoming was still frontier land. In 1867 the railroad reached what is now Cheyenne. Then towns sprang up — Laramie, Rawlins, Rock Springs. Cheyenne, growing rapidly, became the state capital.

There is much in Wyoming to remind you of its frontier past. Cowboys still drive herds of cattle over wide, grassy plains. Thousands of sheep graze on great open ranges. Rodeos and roundups are held every July in Cheyenne.

Long ago the Cheyenne Indians soaked twigs in puddles of oil on the ground. Presto! They had torches. They did not know that someday oil wells would rise above these puddles, bringing up enough oil to fill millions of barrels a year.

Wyoming is rich in other natural resources, too. About five million tons of soft coal are mined each year. Natural gas, coal, iron ore, and clay, as well as many less well-known minerals, are taken from the ground. And in 1963 the discovery of uranium near Rock Springs sent prospectors hurrying to the state with their Geiger counters.

It's easy to understand why tourists are Wyoming's second largest industry. They come for the sport and the scenery — for the big game hunting and the dude ranches, and for the awe-inspiring beauty of the national parks.

![Old North Church steeple]

Old North Church is one of many
historic landmarks in Boston

New England

Toolmaker at work. New England was the
birthplace of American manufacturing.

A covered bridge built in Maine over 100 years ago.

Sugaring in Vermont. Sap from the maple is made into syrup and candy.

Fisherman mends net. Fleets of trawlers fish with these big nets.

Historic moment at Groton, Conn.—launching of the first atomic submarine, the *Nautilus*, in 1954.

The port of New York on a quiet day.

Middle Atlantic States

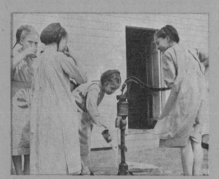

Customs of Pennsylvania Amish people have not changed much over the years.

A ship going through one of the locks of the 2,342-mile St. Lawrence Seaway.

Clothes begin with patterns. New York
leads in manufacture of clothes.

Pittsburgh is one of the nation's
chief steel-making cities.

New Jersey raises many vegetables
for the markets of nearby cities.

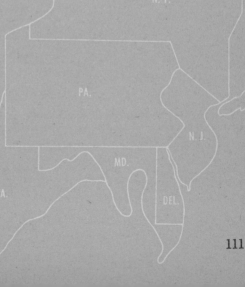

N. Y.

PA.

N. J.

MD.

W. VA.

DEL.

Many boys and girls in the Middle
West raise prize livestock.

Michigan Boulevard in Chicago,
first city of the Middle West.

Middle West

Farm machinery, like this combine, is needed on the huge wheat fields of Kansas.

Famous Wisconsin cheese
is stored to ripen.

On a Detroit assembly line today —
on the nation's roads tomorrow.

A stern-wheeler begins its journey down the Mississippi.

Southern States

In Louisiana, cypress trees and oil wells rise side by side.

A mechanical cotton picker works fast in a Mississippi cotton field.

Kentucky's famous thoroughbred horses.

114

Spraying a grove of citrus trees.

Texas cattle moving to the summer range.

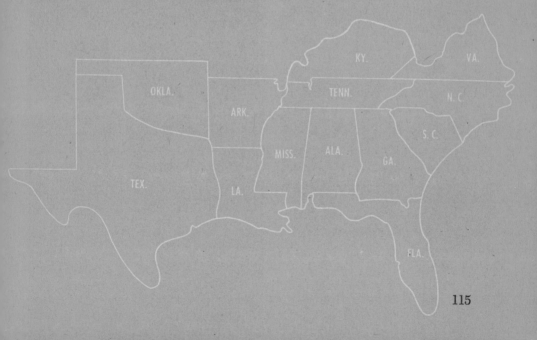

A cowboy ropes a calf at a Wyoming rodeo.

Mountain
States

The falcon is the mascot of the
U.S. Air Force Academy in Colo.

The saguaro cactus may grow 50 feet tall.

A prospector collects uranium ore samples in New Mexico.

Hoover Dam is shared by Arizona and Nevada.

A giant tree will soon begin its journey to an Oregon sawmill.

Pacific Coast

Sand dunes in Death Valley.

Pineapples, one of Hawaii's big crops, are harvested by modern machinery.

This Eskimo's kayak is made of wood and sealskin. Scene: Alaska.

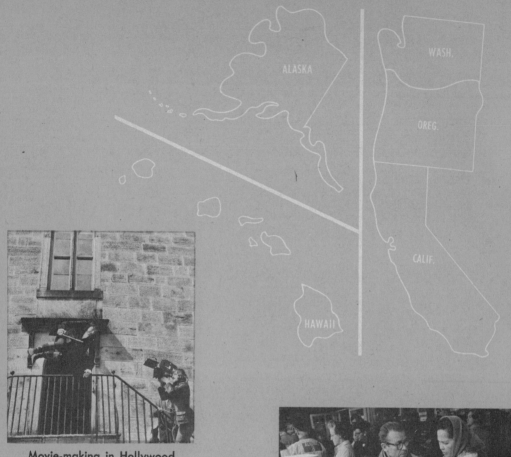

Movie-making in Hollywood.

Fishing for salmon with hoop nets on the Columbia River.

Fresh crabs are a favorite at Fisherman's Wharf in San Francisco.

119

DID YOU KNOW
THAT IN THE U.S...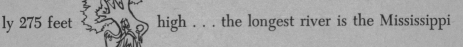

"General Sherman" is a California tree, 3,500 years old and near-

ly 275 feet high . . . the longest river is the Mississippi

(2,348 miles) . . . the largest city is New York City . . . the coldest spot

is Tanana, Alaska . . . the largest active volcano

is Mauna Loa in Hawaii . . . the largest natural bridge is Rainbow

Bridge in Utah . . . our largest lake is Lake Superior° . . .

°The largest of the Great Lakes, Lake Superior, is also bounded by Canada.

the wettest spot is Mt. Waileale in Hawaii (record: 642 inches of

rain in one year) . . . our smallest state is Rhode Island

. . . the largest man-made hole is the open-pit

mine at Mesabi, Minnesota . . . the widest glacier is Malaspina

Glacier in Alaska . . . the lowest point is Death Valley, California

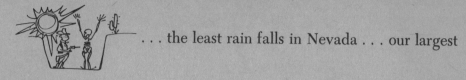 . . . the least rain falls in Nevada . . . our largest

and oldest national park is Yellowstone National Park . . . the most

peanuts 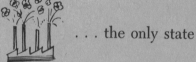 are raised in Georgia . . . our largest desert

is Mojave, California . . . our largest state is Alaska . . . the largest

popcorn processing plant is in Iowa . . . the only state

pronounced as one syllable is Maine and Ask, Me., is a town there

. . . some towns are named for chemicals—Carbon, Calcium, Cobalt

and Soda . . . the largest silver mine is in

Idaho . . . our oldest town is St. Augustine, Florida . . . the highest

mountain is Mt. McKinley in Alaska (20,320 feet) . . . the highest

waterfall is Yosemite Falls in California

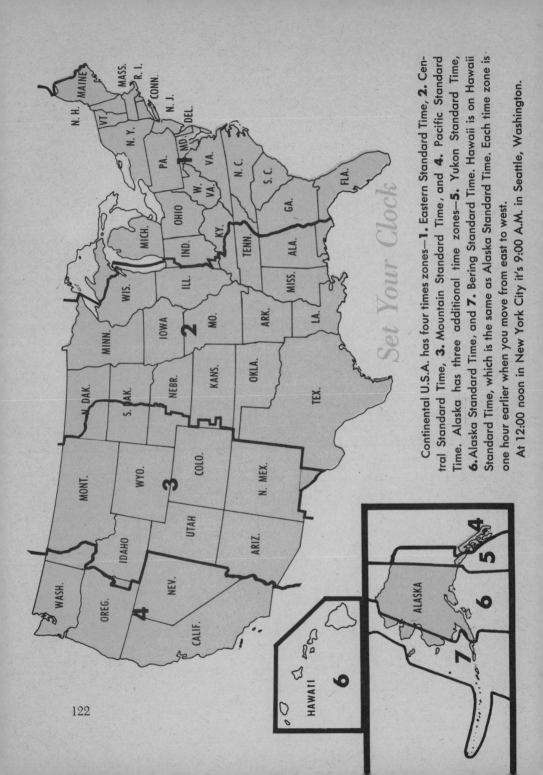

Set Your Clock

Continental U.S.A. has four times zones—**1.** Eastern Standard Time, **2.** Central Standard Time, **3.** Mountain Standard Time, and **4.** Pacific Standard Time. Alaska has three additional time zones—**5.** Yukon Standard Time, **6.** Alaska Standard Time, and **7.** Bering Standard Time. Hawaii is on Hawaii Standard Time, which is the same as Alaska Standard Time. Each time zone is one hour earlier when you move from east to west.

At 12:00 noon in New York City it's 9:00 A.M. in Seattle, Washington.

STATE BIRDS AND FLOWERS

ALABAMA	Yellowhammer	Camellia
ALASKA	Willow Ptarmigan	Forget-me-not
ARIZONA	Cactus Wren	Saguaro Cactus
ARKANSAS	Mockingbird	Apple Blossom
CALIFORNIA	Valley Quail	Golden Poppy
COLORADO	Lark Bunting	Columbine
CONNECTICUT	Robin	Mountain Laurel
DELAWARE	Blue Hen Chicken	Peach Blossom
FLORIDA	Mockingbird	Orange Blossom
GEORGIA	Brown Thrasher	Cherokee Rose
HAWAII	Hawaiian Goose	Hibiscus
IDAHO	Mountain Bluebird	Lewis Mock Orange
ILLINOIS	Cardinal	Violet
INDIANA	Cardinal	Peony
IOWA	Eastern Goldfinch	Wild Rose
KANSAS	Western Meadowlark	Sunflower
KENTUCKY	Cardinal	Goldenrod
LOUISIANA	Brown Pelican	Magnolia
MAINE	Chickadee	White Pine Cone and Tassel
MARYLAND	Baltimore Oriole	Black-eyed Susan
MASSACHUSETTS	Chickadee	Mayflower
MICHIGAN	Robin	Apple Blossom
MINNESOTA	Loon	Showy Lady's-slipper
MISSISSIPPI	Mockingbird	Magnolia
MISSOURI	Bluebird	Hawthorn
MONTANA	Western Meadowlark	Bitterroot
NEBRASKA	Western Meadowlark	Goldenrod
NEVADA	Mountain Bluebird	Sagebrush
NEW HAMPSHIRE	Purple Finch	Purple Lilac
NEW JERSEY	Eastern Goldfinch	Violet
NEW MEXICO	Road Runner	Yucca
NEW YORK	Bluebird	Rose
NORTH CAROLINA	Cardinal	Flowering Dogwood
NORTH DAKOTA	Western Meadowlark	Wild Prairie Rose
OHIO	Cardinal	Scarlet Carnation
OKLAHOMA	Scissor-tailed Flycatcher	Mistletoe
OREGON	Western Meadowlark	Oregon Grape
PENNSYLVANIA	Ruffed Grouse	Mountain Laurel
RHODE ISLAND	Rhode Island Red	Violet
SOUTH CAROLINA	Carolina Wren	Yellow Jessamine
SOUTH DAKOTA	Ring-necked Pheasant	Pasqueflower
TENNESSEE	Mockingbird	Iris
TEXAS	Mockingbird	Bluebonnet
UTAH	Gull	Sego Lily
VERMONT	Hermit Thrush	Red Clover
VIRGINIA	Cardinal	Flowering Dogwood
WASHINGTON	Willow Goldfinch	Coast Rhododendron
WEST VIRGINIA	Cardinal	Rhododendron
WISCONSIN	Robin	Violet
WYOMING	Meadowlark	Indian Paintbrush

The official flower of District of Columbia is American Beauty Rose; its bird, Wood Thrush.

HOW MANY?

STATE	POPULATION*	REPRESENTATIVES	ELECTORAL VOTES	STATE	POPULATION*	REPRESENTATIVES	ELECTORAL VOTES
Alabama	3,444,165	7	9	Montana	694,409	2	4
Alaska	302,173	1	3	Nebraska	1,483,791	3	5
Arizona	1,772,482	4	6	Nevada	488,738	1	3
Arkansas	1,923,295	4	6	New Hampshire	737,681	2	4
California	19,953,134	43	45	New Jersey	7,168,164	15	17
Colorado	2,207,259	5	7	New Mexico	1,016,000	2	4
Connecticut	3,032,217	6	8	New York	18,241,266	39	41
Delaware	548,104	1	3	North Carolina	5,082,059	11	13
D.C.	756,510	0	3	North Dakota	617,761	1	3
Florida	6,789,443	15	17	Ohio	10,652,017	23	25
Georgia	4,589,575	10	12	Oklahoma	2,559,253	6	8
Hawaii	769,913	2	4	Oregon	2,091,385	4	6
Idaho	713,008	2	4	Pennsylvania	11,793,909	25	27
Illinois	11,113,976	24	26	Rhode Island	949,723	2	4
Indiana	5,193,669	11	13	South Carolina	2,590,516	6	8
Iowa	2,825,041	6	8	South Dakota	666,257	2	4
Kansas	2,249,071	5	7	Tennessee	3,924,164	8	10
Kentucky	3,219,311	7	9	Texas	11,196,730	24	26
Louisiana	3,643,180	8	10	Utah	1,059,273	2	4
Maine	993,663	2	4	Vermont	444,732	1	3
Maryland	3,922,399	8	10	Virginia	4,648,494	10	12
Massachusetts	5,689,170	12	14	Washington	3,409,169	7	9
Michigan	8,875,083	19	21	West Virginia	1,744,237	4	6
Minnesota	3,805,069	8	10	Wisconsin	4,417,933	9	11
Mississippi	2,216,912	5	7	Wyoming	332,416	1	3
Missouri	4,677,399	10	12				

*According to the U.S. Census Bureau's 1970 figures.

HOW AMERICA GREW

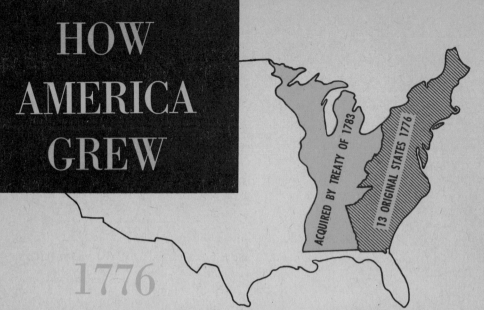

1776

13 original states: Mass., N.H., R.I., Conn., N.J., Del., N.Y., Pa., Md., Va., N.C., S.C., Ga. **Treaty of 1783 became:** Ohio, Ind., Ill., Mich., Wis., Ky., Tenn., Miss., Ala.

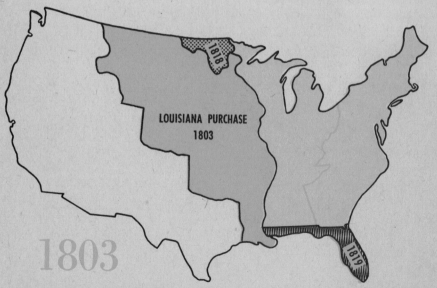

1803

Louisiana Purchase became: La., Iowa, Mo., Ark., Nebr., S. Dak., parts of Okla., Kans., N. Dak., Mont., Wyo., Colo., Minn. **1818:** Territory ceded by Great Britain became: part of N. Dak., Minn. **1819:** Florida Purchase (from Spain).

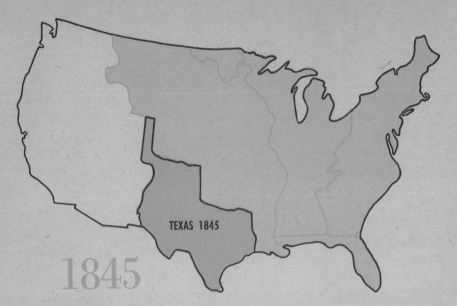

TEXAS 1845

1845

Texas Annexation became: Tex., part of Kans., Okla., N. Mex., Colo., Wyo.

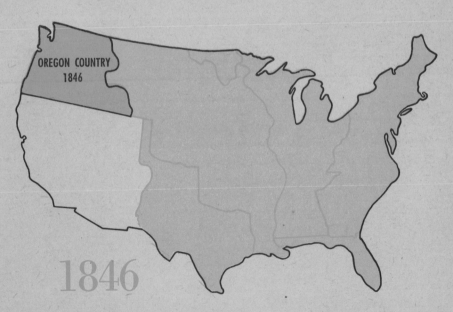

OREGON COUNTRY 1846

1846

Oregon Country Annexation became: Oreg., Wash., Idaho, part of Mont., Wyo.

MEXICAN CESSION 1848

GADSDEN
PURCHASE 1853

1848

Mexican Cession became: Calif., Nev., Ariz., part of Colo., Wyo., N. Mex.
Gadsden Purchase from Mexico became: part of N. Mex., Ariz.

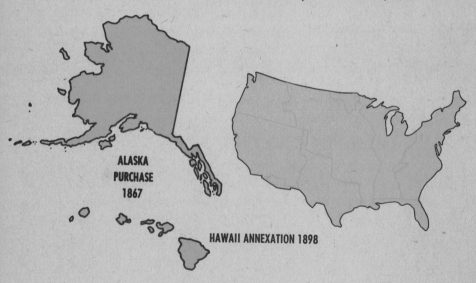

ALASKA
PURCHASE
1867

HAWAII ANNEXATION 1898

In 1959 the U.S. admitted Alaska and Hawaii to statehood.

FIFTY STATES—ONE NATION

The Great Seal of the United States

Our nation's motto tells that we are fifty states united. The Latin words on the Great Seal—E PLURIBUS UNUM—mean *from many — one.*

The other parts of the Great Seal have special meaning, too. The eagle represents the United States. The arrows stand for the power of Congress to declare war. The olive branch stands for the hope of peace. Above the eagle's head are thirteen stars for the thirteen original states.

The Great Seal is used on important government documents.